T0018019

THE MYSTERIOUS LIFE OF
DR BARRY

A SURGEON UNLIKE
ANY OTHER

HOW DR BARRY BROKE THE RULES

©YellowBelly photography

Lisa Williamson has loved history ever since she was small, and at school it was her favourite subject. In year nine, she studied the history of medicine and has remained fascinated by the (often bizarre) procedures once used to treat illness and disease.

Upon leaving school, Lisa was torn between pursuing a degree in history or drama. She ended up going for drama and worked as an actor for over a decade before turning to writing.

Lisa is the bestselling author of *The Art of Being Normal*, a YA story about the friendship between a trans girl and a gay boy described as 'a life-changing and life-saving book' by Philip Pullman and 'extraordinary' by Non Pratt. She has written two other highly regarded YA novels, *All About Mia* and *Paper Avalanche*.

Her website is www.lisawilliamsonauthor.com

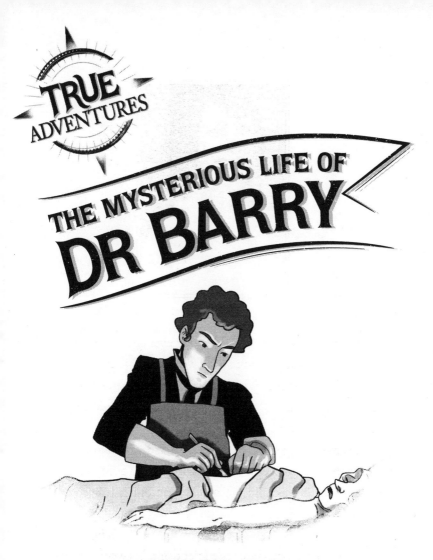

TRUE ADVENTURES

THE MYSTERIOUS LIFE OF
DR BARRY

A SURGEON UNLIKE
ANY OTHER

LISA WILLIAMSON

With illustrations by Amerigo Pinelli

PUSHKIN CHILDREN'S

Pushkin Press
71–75 Shelton Street
London WC2H 9JQ

Text © Lisa Williamson 2020
Illustrations © Amerigo Pinelli 2020

First published in the UK by Pushkin Press in 2020

1 3 5 7 9 8 6 4 2

ISBN 13: 978-1-78269-278-2

Designed and typeset by Tetragon, London
Printed and bound by CPI Group (UK) Ltd, Croydon, CRO 4YY

www.pushkinpress.com

THE MYSTERIOUS LIFE OF
DR BARRY

The British Empire
in the 1860s

Montreal
Cork
Edinburgh
Crimea
Jamaica
Trinidad
St. Helena
Cape Town

PROLOGUE

***

MONDAY 24 JULY 1865

The old woman heaved herself up the narrow stairs, pausing for breath on the landing before pushing the bedroom door open. As she stepped inside, she clasped her hand over her mouth and nose and tried her best not to breathe in. Even though she'd been preparing dead bodies for a living since she was a teenager, she had never quite got used to the pungent smell of death, especially on hot days like this. Keen to get the job over and done with as quickly as possible, she tied a hanky around her face in a bid to block out the terrible stench, rolled up her sleeves and got to work.

The dead man was lying in bed. He was small and slight with pointy features, pale waxy skin and curiously bright red hair. Although he was most definitely deceased, the woman couldn't help but feel a bit nervous at being in such proximity.

Before his retirement, Dr James Barry had held the position of Inspector General of Hospitals, one of the most senior positions in the medical profession. As an Army surgeon, he had travelled the world and achieved worldwide acclaim for performing one of the very first successful Caesarean section operations (delivering a baby by removing it from its mother's womb via an incision to the stomach).

He was equally well known for his ferocious temper. According to the maids downstairs with whom the woman was friendly, Dr Barry's outbursts were both frequent and intense. The legend went that Florence Nightingale (the famous founder of modern nursing) had once found herself on the receiving end of Dr Barry's sharp tongue! There were even rumours he had once fought a duel. However, looking at him now, so pale and frail, it was all rather hard to imagine.

The woman paused to bow her head in a mark of respect before reaching down to carefully peel off his dirty nightshirt.

As she began to wash Dr Barry's skinny body, she noticed something wasn't quite right. She blinked, almost certain she was seeing things before checking again.

She was *not* seeing things.

She staggered backwards in shock, her sponge falling from her fingers.

Although the man's face was definitely that of Dr James Barry, the master of the house, his body was unmistakably female. Unsure quite what to do with this information, the woman had no choice but to complete her task. With trembling hands, she picked up her sponge and, in a daze, cleaned the rest of the body. After wrapping it in its shroud, she stumbled out of the room and into the boiling hot afternoon, her head spinning at what she had just witnessed.

Over the coming weeks, she could think of nothing else. Dr Barry had been one of the highest-ranking surgeons in the British Army. Had he been tricking everyone this entire time? Just the thought made her feel very confused indeed. She agonized over what to do. Was it her business to tell? She suspected it wasn't. At the same time, she had a feeling a story as shocking as this one might be of interest to the press. Times were tough and the bit of cash she could possibly earn from selling Dr Barry's story was all too tempting.

In the end, seduced by the prospect of payment and unable to keep her bizarre and shocking secret to herself any longer, the woman decided to speak out about her discovery, and by the end of August the unbelievable story had been splashed across newspapers all around the globe. The public reaction was a curious mixture of outrage and glee. Was it true? Had a woman *really* managed to successfully

A BOLD PLAN

1809

Margaret Bulkley was eating breakfast when her mother Mary Anne dropped a dirty white envelope on the kitchen table.

'A letter for you,' Mary Anne said in a grim voice. 'Looks like your brother's writing.'

Margaret pulled a face. Her older brother John was not exactly her favourite person. It was his selfish behaviour and spendthrift ways that had brought the once prosperous Bulkley family to the brink of financial ruin, forcing Mary Anne and Margaret to flee their home in Ireland and seek a new start in London. It was thanks to John that instead of the spacious townhouse they had once inhabited in Cork, Margaret and her mother were now sharing a poky set of rooms overlooking Fitzroy Square. It was their fifth home in as many months, and although an improvement on their previous lodgings (a noisy, cramped lodging house in the West End), it was a far cry from the comforts they'd once enjoyed.

'Well, aren't you going to open it?' Mary Anne asked.

'Maybe,' Margaret replied, shrugging as she toyed with the envelope.

Even though she hadn't seen John in the flesh for some years now, the arrival of his letter confirmed that her anger at him had not faded one bit. As a boy, he'd been given opportunity after opportunity, and from what Margaret could work out he'd squandered every single one. It was impossible *not* to feel cross, especially when she knew for a fact she was far cleverer and more interesting than her foolish older brother would ever be.

Margaret didn't open John's letter until after breakfast, taking it up to her bedroom to read in privacy, without her mother peering over her shoulder.

The door shut safely behind her, she settled on her bed and eased the filthy letter from its envelope. As she read, her eyes bulged with fury. John had written the letter from the cramped hold of the *Adriatic*, a ship bound for military action in the West Indies. Apparently he had left his law apprenticeship in

Dublin to become a soldier, and although his letter indicated he now rather regretted his rash decision and was actually quite terrified of what lay ahead, Margaret could barely contain her jealousy.

As a child growing up in Cork, Margaret had longed for adventure. Uninterested in dolls or dressing up or any of the other activities that other little girls her age seemed to enjoy, she spent all of her free time down by the quayside. Her flame-red hair blew in the breeze as she watched the ships come and go, daydreaming about the adventures awaiting the passengers queuing up to board. Some of them were Navy vessels bound for far-flung destinations. The quayside teemed with soldiers looking smart and proud in their scarlet uniforms, brass buttons gleaming as they marched past in perfect unison. Margaret would study them for hours on end, desperately wishing she could join their ranks and march alongside them.

Quaking with annoyance, Margaret tossed John's letter aside and marched over to her desk. She sat down and grabbed a fresh piece of writing paper, a pot of ink and her quill.

'Was I not a girl, I would be a soldier!' she scrawled, leaving angry blots of ink across the page.

But women weren't allowed to be soldiers. In fact, as far as Margaret could make out, women weren't allowed to be anything much at all.

This was a problem. At nineteen, Margaret needed to start bringing in a wage, and soon. Thanks to John's escapades back in Ireland, money was tight and living costs in London were eye-wateringly expensive. For the time being, Margaret and her mother were living off money raised from the sale of works of art painted by Margaret's late uncle (and Mary Anne's older brother), the renowned painter James Barry. However, the auction had not risen anywhere near the amount hoped for and Margaret was painfully aware that it would not last for ever. More importantly, she was desperate to escape from under her mother's roof and make her own way in life.

However, the choice of careers available to girls like Margaret wasn't exactly inspiring. Margaret's cleverness, quick wit and charisma were remarked upon by almost everyone she met, but her gender and lack of social status meant that the very best she could hope for was a position as a governess in a well-to-do household, and although Margaret liked children well enough, the prospect of spending the rest of her life looking after other people's offspring bored her to tears.

In her spare time, Margaret devoured every book she could get her hands on, studied the globe, learned French and practised her penmanship and grammar. She *knew* she possessed a good brain, perhaps even an exceptional one. Oh, if only she had the chance to use it!

Margaret shoved her letter into an envelope and headed out to post it.

'I'll come with you if you like,' Mary Anne volunteered.

'No thank you,' Margaret replied. 'I want to be by myself for a bit.'

Her mother walked far too slowly for Margaret's liking and would also only want to know what she had written. No, Margaret wanted to stew alone.

She posted her letter, but instead of heading straight home, decided to go for a walk. It was a nice day, bright and not too chilly, and she hoped the buzz of the city she was slowly learning to call 'home' would cheer her up a bit.

As usual, she found herself gravitating towards the gates of the Middlesex Hospital on Mortimer Street, one of the most important medical schools in the city. Her thoughts of John melted away as she watched, transfixed, as hundreds of young men around her age flooded in and out of the grand building, armed with important-looking books and polished wooden cases carrying surgical instruments. In a few years' time, the most talented of these students might be surgeons, commanding impressive salaries. For the second time that day, Margaret found herself overcome with envy. If given the chance, she was certain she could compete with these men, no problem.

Of all the books she had read, it was those on science and medicine that had truly captured her imagination. Unfortunately, along with the Army, a career as a doctor was firmly off limits for the female sex, no matter how clever they were, and it looked unlikely that was going to change anytime soon.

After over an hour of loitering at the gates, Margaret reluctantly tore herself away and trudged home. Instead of raising her spirits, her walk had left her feeling even more despondent than ever and she remained in a bad mood for the rest of the day.

Later that evening, as they sat by the fire after dinner, needlework on their laps, Margaret complained to her mother about the unfairness of it all.

'It's just so stupid,' she said, tossing aside her (rather untidy) embroidery ring and folding her arms across her chest. 'I don't care what people say – I'm as clever as any man.'

'Of course you are, darling,' Mary Anne said soothingly. 'But short of disguising yourself as one, there's nothing much we can do about it.' She chuckled and returned her attention to her sewing.

'Wait a second, what did you say?' Margaret asked.

Mary Anne looked up, a slight frown on her face. 'I said, short of disguising yourself as a man, there's nothing much we can do about it,' she repeated uncertainly. 'Why?'

'That's it,' Margaret said, leaping to her feet, her voice bubbling with excitement.

'That's what?' an utterly confused Mary Anne asked.

'I'm far too brainy to waste my life cooped up in some stuffy nursery teaching some snotty-nosed kids their ABCs,' Margaret said. 'I know I can't *be* a man, but maybe I can do something just as good.'

'And what's that?'

A huge grin spread across Margaret's face. 'Simple, Mother. Exactly what you suggested. If I can't be a man, then I'll *pretend* to be one.'

Margaret went to bed that night, her head buzzing with possibilities. It was an outlandish plan, make no mistake, but maybe, just maybe, she had the brains and daring to pull it off.

The next day she plucked up the courage to run it by Dr Fryer and General Miranda, close friends of her late uncle, James Barry. Dr Edward Fryer was a doctor by trade but his first love was literature. Upon meeting Margaret on her arrival in London as a plucky fourteen-year-old, he noted her fierce intelligence and thirst for knowledge and made it his mission to expand her educational horizons. General Don Francisco de Miranda meanwhile was a military leader and celebrated revolutionary with grand plans to liberate his home country, Venezuela. Like Fryer, Miranda agreed Margaret had something special and gave her access to his vast library. As a result of their commitment to her education, Margaret had grown to trust them implicitly.

'Well?' Margaret said, once she'd finished speaking. 'What do you think?'

There was a long pause. Margaret held her breath, her fingers crossed in the pocket of her skirts.

Fryer spoke first. 'I understand your frustrations, Margaret,' he said slowly. 'But this seems rather extreme, not to mention dangerous.'

'That's what I said!' Mary Anne yelped from where she was seated in the corner of the room.

Margaret whirled around to face her. 'Mother, this has nothing to do with you,' she said.

'I beg to differ,' Mary Anne replied. 'Exactly whose funds will you be relying on to carry out this ridiculous plan, hmm? From where I'm standing, this has *everything* to do with me.'

Margaret sighed. Ever since she had come up with her plan, her mother had been doing everything in her power to talk her out of it. She'd done her best to dissuade her mother from coming along today, but alas, Mary Anne had insisted.

'Your mother is right to be cautious,' Fryer said. 'It will take years for you to qualify as a doctor. Are you suggesting you'll be able to maintain a disguise for all that time? I don't mean to be a killjoy but you're barely five feet tall!'

'So?' Margaret said. 'Not all men are giants.'

'It's not just about your height, Margaret. Surely the university will carry out checks. What if they ask to see your birth certificate?'

'We'll say I lost it on the boat over from Ireland.'

'What about the other students? And your professors? You'll have to convince every single one of them. The slightest hint of suspicion could have disastrous consequences!'

'I'd be careful,' Margaret said.

Fryer continued to list his concerns and Margaret had an answer for every single one. However, Fryer still wasn't entirely convinced.

'See!' Mary Anne cried triumphantly. 'I told you it was a terrible idea!'

Margaret turned to General Miranda in desperation. Famed for his radical tactics, she was hopeful he might be on board.

'Well?' she said.

There was a pause before he spoke. Margaret held her breath once again.

'I think it's genius!' Miranda bellowed. 'Utter genius!'

Margaret beamed.

'But, Miranda,' Fryer said. 'What if Margaret is found out?'

'What if she *isn't*?' General Miranda replied. 'You constantly talk of how brilliant her brain is – surely you must agree it would be criminal to let it go to waste?'

Fryer hesitated and Margaret felt a surge of hope.

'Please,' she said. 'Let me at least try. It's not like I've got anything to lose.'

This wasn't strictly true. Margaret wasn't exactly sure what the penalty would be for a woman impersonating a man, but she was fairly certain such a bold stunt wouldn't be looked upon kindly. However, now wasn't the time to say this out loud, especially with her mother in the room. A naturally nervous woman at the best of times, Mary Anne had already worked herself into a state of anxiety and the last thing Margaret wanted to do was give her any further ammunition. As Mary Anne had correctly pointed out, Margaret was relying on the last of her mother's money to fund the audacious plan. The last thing she wanted to do was highlight the possible risks.

'Please,' she repeated. 'I'll make it work, I promise, and if I don't, you have the right to tell me "I told you so" until the end of time.'

'What do you say, Fryer?' Miranda asked, his eyes twinkling. 'Are you in or not?'

'If I'm not, you'll just go ahead anyway, won't you?' Fryer said.

'Yes,' Margaret and Miranda replied in unison.

He let out a heavy sigh. 'In that case, I suppose I must be in.'

Margaret and Miranda's hoots of delight drowned out Mary Anne's wail of anguish.

Ignoring her, Margaret, Miranda and Fryer wasted no time in hatching a plan. It was decided that Margaret would follow in Fryer's own footsteps and enrol at medical school in Edinburgh. There, she was less likely to bump into anyone she knew and risk being exposed.

'But what about *after* medical school?' Mary Anne wanted to know. 'What then?'

It was a valid point. Would Margaret simply pretend to be a man for ever? She wasn't even twenty – she had her whole life ahead of her. What about marriage? And children?

'I know!' Miranda said, banging his fist down so loudly on the table it made everyone jump. 'She can practise in Venezuela.'

It would only be a matter of time before he returned and liberated the country.

'Under my new regime, women will be free to practise medicine,' Miranda declared. 'Margaret will be a trailblazer!'

Even better! Not only would Margaret get to be

a doctor, but she would also get to travel across the Atlantic Ocean and embark on exactly the sort of adventure she'd been longing for, ever since she was a child. It was the perfect solution.

There was just one (fairly significant) hitch.

She had to get through medical school first.

PLEASED TO MEET YOU

November

Margaret opened her eyes. The rug under her feet was covered with clumps of red hair.

Her hair.

Gingerly, she reached up and stroked her shorn skull. She swallowed hard. After months of talking and planning and plotting late into the night, it was finally happening.

The following morning, she and her mother would be boarding a boat bound for Edinburgh – and Margaret's brand-new life as a medical student.

'Are you sure about this?' Mary Anne asked for about the thousandth time. She'd finally stopped crying at the sight of her daughter's cropped hair.

'It's a bit late to ask that now, don't you think?' Margaret quipped.

Mary Anne didn't laugh. Instead, she bent down and picked up a lock of Margaret's hair, her eyes glossy with fresh tears.

Margaret sighed. 'Enough of this sentimentality, Mother,' she said. 'I'm doing this for both of us, remember?'

'I know, I know,' Mary Anne replied, blotting her face with a handkerchief. 'I'm just nervous, that's all.'

'Me too,' Margaret said, taking both her mother's hands in hers. 'But if this is going to work, we need to be strong. Both of us.'

Mary Anne managed a small nod but continued to look terrified.

Margaret let her gaze drift over her mother's shoulder, falling on the clothes laid out neatly on her bed. Over the past few weeks, an entire male wardrobe had been purchased, from socks and underwear, to hats and gloves. It hadn't been a straightforward task. At just five foot tall, Margaret was significantly shorter than most men and almost every garment they'd acquired had had to be tailored to fit her small, slender frame.

She'd tried everything on individually but this would be the first time she'd worn her disguise in its entirety. She waited until Mary Anne had left the room before completing her transformation. Her heart beating wildly, she stepped out of her dress, kicking it under her bed out of sight. She then took a deep breath and slowly, carefully, began to put on her new clothes, her fingers fumbling over the unfamiliar fastenings. She waited until the final button was done up before daring to look at her reflection in the mirror.

She blinked, unable to quite process what she was seeing.

She looked like a stranger. Only the stranger had her face. It was both incredibly spooky, and oddly hypnotic. Was this really the image that was going to greet her every time she looked in the mirror for the next three years?

Three years.

It seemed like such a long stretch.

A knock at the door made her flinch.

'Come in,' she called.

Mary Anne slid back into the room, her hands flying to her mouth as she gasped at the sight of her only daughter. 'Oh, Margaret!' she cried, clutching her chest, her eyes brimming with tears. 'My little girl!'

'No,' Margaret said sternly, wagging her finger. 'I'm not Margaret any more, remember? Or your daughter, for that matter. I'm your nephew now. James. James Barry.'

The name had been selected in tribute to Margaret's late uncle.

THE FIRST TEST

James stepped out into the dreary November afternoon, his heart hammering wildly in his chest. This was the first time he'd left the house dressed as a man, and as he descended the steps, his head lowered, the enormity of what he was doing truly hit him.

Before any of the neighbours could spot him, he dived into the waiting carriage, Mary Anne scuttling close behind. It simply wouldn't do for his disguise to be uncovered within just moments of his leaving his front door.

'Let's go,' he called to the driver.

He winced at how feminine he sounded. No matter how hard he tried to deepen his voice, it sounded as high and girlish as ever. He only hoped it wouldn't be the thing to give him away.

With a jerk, the carriage pulled away from the kerb. At the last moment, James dared to peer out of the window and bid a final goodbye to his most recent home. Opposite him, Mary Anne stared straight ahead, her back rigid, her pale blue eyes full of terror. Despite all the careful planning and preparation, she remained as nervous about the scheme as ever.

'It'll be OK, Mother,' James said, leaning across to give her knee a reassuring squeeze. 'Just trust me.'

He only wished he felt as confident as he sounded. The fact was, he was probably just as terrified as his mother. Yes, they were ploughing the last of Mary Anne's savings into paying for James's fees, but if they got found out, *he* was the one who would have to face the music. Still, there was no point in dwelling on the risks. If he was going to pull this off, he needed to hold his nerve and take things one step at a time.

Although James had been living in London for six years at this point, the journey to the docks took him through parts of the city he'd never visited before – Whitechapel and Clerkenwell – neighbourhoods where poverty and hardship were rife. For a short while, James forgot his own worries as he peered out at the grimy streets with their dilapidated buildings and disease-ravaged inhabitants. Although James was by no means rich, he'd always had a roof over his head and plenty to eat. The idea that people lived in such squalid conditions made him squirm with discomfort. It just seemed so unfair. Why should some people suffer, while others wanted for nothing?

There and then, he made a decision about his future.

'I'm going to help them,' he said out loud, waking Mary Anne from her nap.

'You're going to what?' she said dozily.

He pointed out the window. 'When I'm qualified. I'm going to do my best to use my position and knowledge to help disadvantaged people; really make a difference.'

'*If*,' Mary Anne reminded him. '*If* you qualify.'

'Oh, I'll qualify,' James said, jutting out his chin. 'Just you wait and see.'

The carriage eventually shuddered to a stop in Wapping, where James and Mary Anne were to board the ship to Scotland.

James trembled with nerves as he approached the ship although he did his best to hide them for his mother's sake. Even with his new haircut and men's clothes, he knew he cut a strange figure. At barely five foot tall and naturally slim, he was noticeably small, especially compared to the other male passengers, all of whom seemed to loom over him. James had spent the past few months practising how to compensate for his small stature by observing the movements of General Miranda.

Tall and sturdy, yet graceful and elegant, Miranda was the perfect subject. However, there was a big difference between imitating Miranda behind closed doors and doing it for real in front of a bunch of strangers. James took a moment to collect himself, then rolled back his shoulders, puffed out his chest, and with one hand behind his back, took big confident strides down to the gangway, all the way to the male cabin he'd be sleeping in for the next four nights.

By the time he reached the door, he was sweating profusely. He paused as he considered what was on the other side. He'd never shared a bedroom in his life, never mind with a load of strange men. Unfortunately, there was no alternative. He could hardly sleep in a female cabin in his current get-up.

He took a deep breath and pushed open the door. The cabin revealed itself to be large but cramped, the bunks crammed disturbingly close together. James identified an empty bunk in the far corner and made a beeline for it. As he passed, a few of the other inhabitants glanced up from their reading or card games but no one seemed especially interested in their new cabin mate, barely giving him a second look. James sank onto the hard mattress, his heart hammering in his chest.

That was when the smell hit him. The ship hadn't set off yet and the cabin already stank to high heaven of smelly men. James wrinkled his nose and tried his best not to breathe in.

It was going to be a *long* five days.

The voyage was not exactly a relaxing one. Although it was soon clear his cabin mates had little interest in him, James remained eager to avoid their company and the stinky cabin as much as possible. He spent his days playing endless games of cards with Mary Anne in the passenger lounge or roaming the deck, daydreaming about his future life in Venezuela. At night, he waited until the last possible moment to return to the cabin, diving into bed fully clothed and barely sleeping a wink.

He took care not to share his anxieties with Mary Anne, fearful that if he did, she'd put a stop to the entire scheme and have them on the first ship back to London.

After five days at sea, James was relieved beyond measure when the ship finally docked at Leith in Scotland. As he disembarked, the winter sunshine warming his face, he felt a flutter of excitement in his belly.

The first test was over and he'd passed it.

Unfortunately, many more much tougher tests lay ahead.

A PROMISING YOUNG MAN

'Come in!' boomed a deep, gruff voice.

James took a deep breath and pushed open the heavy wooden door.

All new medical students were required to visit each of their new professors in turn in order to pay the fee required to book seats in their upcoming lectures.

James stepped inside the wood-panelled office and made his way towards the professor who was seated behind an impossibly large desk covered with paperwork.

As James stammered out his request, his body jangled with nerves. He may have successfully fooled his fellow passengers on the voyage from London to

Edinburgh but now he was faced with some of the most brilliant brains in the country – surely *they'd* see through his disguise.

However, the professor in question, a bearded man with stern eyes and a down-turned mouth, barely glanced up, taking James's money, handing him an entrance ticket for the coming term's lectures and sending him on his way.

As the day went on, James was surprised to discover that every other professor he visited seemed equally uninterested in him. Although a few of them noted their new student's dainty stature and smooth skin, not one gave it any further thought. To them, James was just another student, one of hundreds, at this stage all pretty much indistinguishable from the rest.

James returned to the small flat he was sharing with Mary Anne and reported back, his voice breathless with excitement.

'No one even batted an eyelid,' he said gleefully.

'Well, let's hope it stays that way,' Mary Anne replied grimly.

Unlike James, who was growing more confident with every minute that passed, Mary Anne was as fretful and pessimistic as ever, prowling around the flat like a caged animal, just waiting to be found out.

She was particularly distressed the following day when, out of the blue, a letter arrived addressed to James.

'Who's it from?' she asked, wringing her hands as she followed James around the living room. 'It looks official!'

Indeed, neither of them recognized the handwriting on the envelope and as far as they were aware only a small circle of friends knew of their new address in Edinburgh.

'We've been found out, haven't we?' Mary Anne said, her eyes filling with tears. 'I knew it! I just knew it!'

'Shush, Mother!' James said. 'We mustn't jump to conclusions.'

Still, he was nervous as he sliced open the envelope, his eyes widening as he noted the fancy letterhead.

'It's from the Earl of Buchan!' he exclaimed, skimming the first few lines. 'He wants to meet me.'

'The Earl of who?' Mary Anne said.

'Buchan. He's a good friend of Dr Fryer's apparently.'

Mary Anne relaxed a little. She liked Dr Fryer and trusted him not to share their secret.

According to the rest of the letter, the Earl had heard all about James's talents and was keen to meet with the 'promising young man' with the view to possibly sponsoring his studies.

'He wants to meet me for afternoon tea,' James said.

'But what if he realizes?' Mary Anne asked. 'You may have fooled those professors of yours but that was just for a few minutes.'

She had a point. Apart from with his mother, James hadn't had a proper conversation with anyone since arriving in Edinburgh the previous week.

'But I've got to start somewhere,' James said. 'I can't hide away for ever. I'm going to be starting classes soon and meeting all kinds of people.'

Not to mention the fact that the support of a powerful patron (an earl no less) would be *very* welcome indeed.

Mary Anne didn't look convinced.

'How about I speak with Fryer and Miranda and ask them what they think?' James suggested. 'Would that put your mind at rest?'

Mary Anne agreed and James wrote to each of them straightaway. Their responses were unanimously positive, just as he'd hoped. James's instincts were right – Buchan was hugely powerful and respected (not to mention well off) and James would be silly to pass up the opportunity of meeting him and possibly gaining his patronage.

And so it was decided, and a few days later James found himself on the doorstep of Buchan's city residence in the most fashionable part of town.

If the elderly Buchan was troubled by James's slightly unconventional appearance and unusually high voice, he didn't show it, welcoming James into his parlour and plying him with tea and cake. Buchan may have been a member of the aristocracy, but he was a warm, friendly man who always did his best to make his guests feel at ease. James was no exception and he quickly relaxed into Buchan's company. For the first time since arriving in Edinburgh, he let down his guard and allowed his natural personality to shine through, quickly charming Buchan with his wit and intelligence. He even dared to crack a few jokes, which to his delight made Buchan roar with laughter.

Elated at the realization that he had won over such a wise and respected gentleman, James felt ready to throw himself into student life.

The following day, he headed off to his very first lecture with a spring in his step. Striding through the city streets, with no need for a chaperone and no cumbersome skirts flapping around his legs, James felt happier than ever before.

A REAL-LIFE DEAD BODY

1810

It was already dark when James joined the small group of young men gathered outside an anonymous-looking house on a narrow cobbled alleyway in the centre of town.

'I've heard he digs the bodies up himself,' one of them said.

'Rubbish!' another claimed. 'He pays a gang of resurrectionists to do the job for him and gets them shipped up from London.'

'I've heard it's Liverpool,' another chipped in.

They were talking about Dr Andrew Fyfe, the university's famed anatomist and dissector. It was outside his house they were standing, waiting for 6 p.m. to strike so they could go inside.

It was January, and James had been in Edinburgh for just over two months. His first lecture had been a terrifying affair. His hands shook the entire time (his notes were hardly legible) and he barely took in a word the professor said. Despite his nerves, his fellow students were too preoccupied with their own studies to pay him any special attention, and as the days went by, James found himself beginning to relax. As one of several hundred first-year students, he discovered it was easy enough to blend into the background if you put your mind to it. Tonight, however, wouldn't be quite so easy.

Having spent a very enjoyable Christmas at Buchan's country estate, James had returned to the city in the New Year and signed up for Dr Fyfe's private course on practical anatomy. For the sum of three guineas, students could have a go at dissecting a real-life dead body. It was famously grim work but James had become increasingly interested in the idea of surgery and wanted in.

Unfortunately, Fyfe could only accommodate a small number of students in his classes, meaning it would be a lot harder for James to avoid unwanted attention.

'Oi! What do you say, Barry?'

James's head snapped up. A fellow student he vaguely recognized from one of his lectures was talking directly to him.

'Reckon?' he repeated uncertainly.

'About where Fyfe gets his bodies?'

'How should I know?' James replied haughtily, turning away from the group.

'Stuck-up thing,' another one of the students muttered, making the others snicker.

James acted like he hadn't heard, bending down and pretending to tie his shoelace for good measure.

It wasn't the case that he didn't have an opinion on the origins of Fyfe's seemingly endless supply of dead bodies, but James knew better than to let his guard down in front of his peers. He was well aware they found him rude but he didn't care. Better to be considered rude than risk being found out. It would only take a single careless comment or other silly slip-up to shatter his goal of becoming a doctor. Besides, he was far more interested in what lay beyond Dr Fyfe's door than in any of the idle chit-chat taking place outside it.

At 6 p.m. on the dot, the door swung open to reveal Dr Fyfe, a tall, thin man with a long face and watery pale blue eyes.

'Come in, come in,' he said, ushering the students inside.

He led them through his living quarters, past his wife and children, to a large room at the back of the house where the dissecting would take place.

James shivered. The room was as cold as an icebox, its fireplace empty. The windows had been whitewashed to keep out prying eyes, the only light source provided by the candles dotted on every available surface. The walls were lined with shelves crammed with books, jars containing goodness-knows-what, and all manner of syringes and saws in a number of sizes.

In the centre of the room stood a table draped with a white sheet, a human body-shaped mound lying beneath it. As the students shuffled in, their chatter ceased and a hush fell.

Dr Fyfe didn't waste any time, striding over to the table and, with a flourish, whipping the sheet away to reveal the corpse of a young woman, her skin pale and waxy with an unpleasant grey tinge. James's eyes widened. He'd never seen an actual dead body before.

Rumour had it that Fyfe's supply of corpses came from London or Liverpool, where men known as 'resurrectionists' would dig up freshly-buried bodies, pack them in salt and ship them up to Edinburgh. Indeed, from the traces of salt on the woman's body, it looked like this had been the case for her.

James couldn't help but wonder how she might have died. She was only young, twenty-five at the most. Quickly, he pushed this thought away. That isn't important any more, he told himself. If he was going to succeed in this line of work, he needed to be able to keep his emotions in check and focus purely on the task in hand.

Aprons and gloves were distributed and the students were split up into pairs and each given a soiled copy of Dr Fyfe's textbook and a set of rather rusty implements – a saw, forceps, scissors, a knife and a scalpel. Each pair was then given a section of the young woman's body to dissect. James and his partner, a plump young man with wide brown eyes who went by the name of Edward, were assigned the right thorax.

'Do you want to do the cutting or shall I?' James asked.

From the look on Edward's (slightly green) face, James got the feeling it was probably better if he took charge of the knife, leaving his partner to refer to the textbook and give instructions.

His heart fluttering with nerves and excitement, James lifted up the knife the way Dr Fyfe had just demonstrated and began to cut through the unexpectedly tough flesh on the side of the woman's chest. As the skin peeled away, blood oozing, Edward promptly slumped to the ground. He wasn't the only one. All around him, James's classmates were dropping like flies.

Undeterred, James removed the textbook from his partner's limp hand and got on with the task alone, fighting the urge to vomit at every step. The smell was horrific and it was hard not to gag.

Two hours later James and his classmates were dismissed.

'Sorry I fainted on you,' Edward said as they poured out into the alleyway, gasping for mouthfuls of fresh air. 'I feel dreadful about it.'

'That's all right,' James said.

'Can I maybe buy you a drink to apologize?'

James hesitated. Edward seemed nice enough, and after such an intense experience, the thought of retreating to a cosy pub for an hour or so was an appealing one, but deep down he knew he couldn't risk getting close to anyone – no matter how friendly they seemed.

'I can't tonight,' he said.

Edward blinked, clearly taken aback by James's bluntness. Still, he didn't appear to be put off and enquired about James's availability for the following evening.

'I don't think so,' James said.

'You're wasting your time,' another one of the students said. 'Barry only mixes with aristocrats, don't you know.'

James blushed. He didn't know how the boy knew about his association with Buchan and had a horrible feeling it might mark him out as a possible target for further unpleasantness.

'I have to go,' he said curtly. 'Goodnight.'

'Night,' Edward said sadly, frowning as James hurried away.

*   *   *

The following evening, James returned to Dr Fyfe's, arriving at six o'clock exactly so he wouldn't have to spend any longer than necessary interacting with the other students. Clearly the first session had scared off a fair few, as the group was noticeably smaller. Despite the fainting incident, Edward had also returned and once more he and James were paired up, this time tackling the dead woman's axilla (her armpit).

The work was even grimmer than it had been the previous day. The dead woman's body was beginning to rot, making her organs slippery and slimy and increasingly difficult to handle. Edward managed not to faint on this occasion but many others slithered to the ground over the course of the session.

'You should have come to the pub last night,' Edward said as yet another student succumbed. 'It was such good fun.'

James didn't reply.

'If pubs aren't your thing, I was thinking of climbing Arthur's Seat this weekend if you fancied joining me?' Edward added.

Arthur's Seat was a large hill overlooking the city and James had been meaning to climb it since arriving in Edinburgh.

'Could you pass me the scalpel please?' he asked, completely ignoring Edward's invitation.

'Oh, yes, of course,' Edward stuttered, his disappointment clear.

47

James rebuffed all of Edward's other attempts at friendly conversation until Edward seemed to get the message and fell silent.

At the end of the class, James grabbed his things and was the first out of the door, keen to avoid any more invitations to the pub or jaunts up to Arthur's Seat. He felt a twinge of guilt but knew it was better this way. There would be time for friends later in life, he was sure of it.

Exhilarated by his experiences in Dr Fyfe's dissection room, James purchased tickets for more and more courses, until his timetable was completely full up. At night, he pored over his books, his light often shining until two or three in the morning. All this hard work soon paid off and he began to attract the attention of his tutors, many of whom singled him out for special recognition. This came at a price. The more James was praised, the more his fellow students decided they didn't like him. The fact that he enjoyed the support of someone as important as the Earl of Buchan didn't help matters either.

'I don't get it,' they'd grumble. 'What has he got that we haven't?'

James was aware of the mounting hostility towards him but chose to ignore it, as well as Mary Anne's pleas that he keep a low profile.

'I'm sorry, Mother, but I won't change my behaviour for anyone's benefit,' James told her. 'Their jealousy is their issue, not mine.'

The fact was, he enjoyed impressing his tutors far too much to consider taking a step back. He'd tasted success and he liked it very much. Who cared how unpopular it made him?

Winter melted into summer. For most of the students, the passing of the chilly Scottish winter came as a relief. For James though, the climbing temperatures were not quite so welcome. His winter clothes helped to conceal his female body. In just shirtsleeves, he would feel far too exposed. With little choice, James continued to wear his winter layers even on the hottest of days. His classmates giggled and pointed, but James did his best not to react, even with sweat dripping down his face and neck.

It was around this time that rumours began to circulate – rumours that almost stopped James's entire university career in its tracks.

A SECRET EXPOSED

1812

At the beginning of his third and final year, James found himself in front of the university senate.

'I'm very sorry, James, but I'm afraid we are unable to allow you to sit your final examinations,' said the Chair of the senate, an elderly man with a gravelly voice and an impressive moustache.

'But why?' James cried.

They couldn't have found out his secret. Could they?

His heartbeat began to quicken as the three men sitting behind the large oak table exchanged lengthy glances.

The Chair cleared his throat. 'It's been brought to our attention that you may be here under false pretences. In short, you are not who you led us to believe you were.'

'Who? Who told you this?' James asked, his mind racing.

He was well aware that the other students were not fond of him, but none had ever given any indication that they suspected his secret.

'That isn't relevant,' the Chair said. 'They were correct to alert us.'

James closed his eyes. This was it, the moment he'd been dreading. He pictured breaking the news he'd been found out to his mother. This would surely finish her.

'We simply can't be seen to be handing out degrees to children,' the Chair continued.

James's eyes snapped open. 'What?'

The Chair repeated what he'd said.

'What on earth are you talking about?' James asked, by now utterly confused.

Another of the men spoke up. 'We have it on good account that you are not a man of twenty as your records state, but a mere boy of no more than twelve years of age.'

James almost burst out laughing. A boy of twelve? Were they serious? He'd never heard anything so ridiculous. At the same time, he felt hopelessly relieved. His secret was still safe!

'You don't actually believe this rubbish, do you?' he asked.

The men exchanged further glances.

'Do you?' James repeated, his voice firmer this time.

The ensuing silence suggested they might.

Quickly, James's relief was overtaken by pure rage. He'd worked *so* hard and been *so* careful – he wasn't about to allow his medical career to be sabotaged by a silly (not to mention false) rumour, not when he was so very close to qualifying.

'But it simply isn't true!' he said, bashing his fist on the table in frustration.

'Perhaps if you supplied us with a birth certificate?' one of the senate members suggested.

'I told you when I enrolled, it was lost at sea,' James said.

'In that case, I'm afraid our hands are tied.'

With no other paperwork to prove the senate wrong, James had no possible way of convincing them to change their minds. He stormed out of the room in a terrible fury. Every penny he and Mary Anne had, it had all been spent on his education. If he didn't graduate, all of this work would have been for nothing and they'd be back at square one, only this time they'd be penniless to boot.

James headed straight to Buchan's house, and upon seeing his sponsor's kindly face, burst into desperate tears.

'There there, dear boy,' Buchan said, patting his

protégé on the head. 'There must be something we can do.'

While James had a cup of tea and calmed down a bit, Buchan sat down and carefully studied the university guidelines.

'Dear boy!' he cried. 'I told you not to worry. I've read the guidelines from cover to cover and there isn't a single reference to age.'

'Really?' James said. 'You're sure?'

'Yes. In fact, I'm going down there right now and I'll tell them so myself.'

Buchan was a powerful and influential man and the senate quickly backed down. Although still suspicious of James's age, they reluctantly agreed to let him sit his final exams. Providing he passed, James could graduate after all.

However, the examination process was going to be no walk in the park. Every exam, including the oral test, was to be conducted in Latin, a language James had only recently begun to learn. Most terrifying of all, the oral examination of his thesis would take place on stage in front of the other fifty-eight candidates. As someone who went out of his way to avoid public speaking, James was horrified at the prospect of being on such clear display.

Also, although he liked to think he'd adapted well to his new male persona during his three years in Edinburgh, his voice was still significantly higher than those of the other students and the source of most of the gossip surrounding him.

In the lead-up to the exam he practised endlessly in front of the mirror, delivering his thesis in as deep a voice as he could manage, until he was exhausted and his throat red raw.

On the day of the oral test, he was word perfect and although his voice still provoked the odd titter, he felt satisfied with his performance. Still annoyed at the senate for almost derailing his medical career, he couldn't resist slipping in a dig at them, inserting the following Greek quotation into his presentation:

Do not consider whether what I say is a young man speaking, but whether my discussion with you is that of a man of understanding.

James passed with flying colours.

After three years of hard work, he was now officially James Barry M.D.

Finally, he could cast aside his disguise and begin a new life in Venezuela.

Unfortunately, fate had other ideas in store.

ADVENTURE ON THE HORIZON

While James had been frantically studying in Edinburgh, the political situation over in Venezuela had changed rapidly. A coup had occurred and General Miranda found himself accused of treason, deported and thrown in jail in Spain with no hope of release.

Upon hearing the news, James was devastated. Firstly, he'd never see his friend and mentor ever again. Secondly, his lifeline was gone. There wasn't a single country in the world that would allow him to practise medicine as a woman. If he wanted to work as a doctor, he had no choice but to remain in role as Dr James Barry, for the time being at least.

*   *   *

Back in London, James tried not to panic and plunged himself into further study while he tried to figure out what to do next.

In Edinburgh, he'd shown a natural talent for surgery in Dr Fyfe's gruesome sessions and he felt it would be a waste not to explore this further. Not to mention the fact that James was a perfectionist – if he was going to be a surgeon, he wanted to be the best he could possibly be.

At considerable expense, he signed up to study with Astley Cooper, one of the most famous and well-respected surgeons in London. Back in 1801 Astley had famously dissected an elephant in an open-air dissecting theatre and had enjoyed celebrity status ever since.

The moment he set eyes on Cooper, James was utterly star-struck. Charismatic, gifted, and a *very* snappy dresser, Cooper cut an impressive figure and James was determined to curry his favour. However, this wasn't going to be easy. There were one hundred other students on the course, all of them no doubt equally keen to make their mark. At every opportunity, James raised his hand or volunteered to assist, ignoring his fellow students' tuts and all-too-familiar mutters of 'teacher's pet'.

Once more, rumours began to circulate. However, James's time as a medical student was risky for a second, perhaps more deadly reason. A combination of foul air and a confined space made operating theatres incredibly dangerous places to be hanging about in. The risk of disease and infection was rife and medical students fell ill regularly. Indeed, a classmate of James's even died, having contracted pulmonary tuberculosis while studying under Cooper. Many students avoided dissections altogether, choosing to learn about anatomy from their textbooks instead.

James, however, would do nothing of the sort and attended every session without fail, regardless of the risk to his life. He kept himself as healthy as possible, avoiding alcohol, drugs and smoking, and adopting a vegetarian diet. Cooper was suitably impressed, declaring that his young student was clearly destined for great things.

Despite his disappointment at not being able to travel to Venezuela, James was happy to be back in London. Inspired by the elegantly dressed Cooper, James began to pay close attention to fashion, spending all his spare cash on a new wardrobe – silk stockings, boots with stacked heels and a padded frock coat. It was a look that suited James's slender figure and for perhaps the first time since he had set off for Edinburgh three years earlier, he began to feel comfortable in his own skin.

James was considering signing up for yet another course when his mother dropped a bombshell. They'd finally run out of money. Further study was impossible – James would have to find a job.

And fast.

He considered his options. One was to move to the countryside and set up as a private doctor. His mother (unsurprisingly) liked this idea very much, but just the thought of it bored James to tears.

'Please, James,' Mary Anne begged him.

'Sorry, Mother, but I can't. I haven't gone to all this hard work and trouble to spend my days in some sleepy village in the middle of nowhere treating old ladies' bunions day in day out.'

'But you've got to do something,' she said. 'We're as good as destitute.'

That was when James remembered the words he'd written to his brother all those years ago: '*Was I not a girl, I would be a soldier.*'

His eyes lit up.

'What? What is it?' Mary Anne asked in a panic (she knew her child well enough to understand what this expression meant). 'What mad scheme are you cooking up now?'

James just grinned. 'Wait and see, Mother. Wait and see.'

He kissed her on the cheek, grabbed his hat and thundered down the stairs.

Half an hour later he presented himself at the office of the Army Medical Board in Piccadilly and asked to sign up as an Army surgeon.

'How old are you?' the officer behind the desk

asked, looking James up and down, a sceptical expression on his face.

In truth, James was now twenty-four, but thanks to his smooth face and diminutive stature he looked more like fourteen. In the end he plumped for somewhere in the middle, crossed his fingers behind his back and hoped for the best.

'I'm eighteen,' he said, in the gruffest voice he could manage.

'Hmm,' the officer said, clearly not convinced. However, he wasn't exactly in a position to turn the new recruit away – the nation was at war on several fronts and Army doctors were in high demand. Reluctantly, the officer stamped 'approved' on James's application and progressed him to the next stage of the recruitment process – an assessment by the Royal College of Surgeons.

James was not alone in choosing this path. He arrived at the college's headquarters in Lincoln's Inn Fields to discover he was one of over thirty young men hoping to be assessed that day.

James was at the bottom of the list and so faced a tense wait as one by one his fellow applicants were called in to be interviewed.

The interview itself was a famously intense process. Nine examiners were assembled to quiz the candidates on all aspects of surgery and anatomy. Together they were such an intimidating presence that it was not uncommon for the young prospective surgeons to freeze or completely clam up during questioning. Some had even been known to faint.

When his time came, James, although nervous, answered all his questions with ease, and left a few hours later clutching a certificate from the college deeming him 'fit and capable to exercise the Art of Science of Surgery'.

The following day James returned to the Army Medical Board.

'Right,' the administrator said. 'All the paperwork is in order, we just need to get you examined and you'll be all finished.'

'Examined?' James said, panic rising in his chest.

'Yes,' the administrator said. 'All new recruits must undergo a physical examination.'

Although James had been living as a man for over four years by this point, he knew there was no way he could get through a physical examination without being rumbled. Luckily, he had done his homework.

'I'm to be an officer,' he said, rolling back his shoulders and puffing out his chest. 'And I've been reliably informed that anyone of officer class is exempt.'

James was correct. As an officer, he was considered a gentleman and therefore his word alone was deemed sufficient to certify he was fit and well.

The administrator went back to his paperwork. 'My apologies, Mr Barry, you are absolutely right – no examination will be necessary.'

And with that, it was official – James was a doctor in the British Army.

When he turned up at home wearing his uniform, Mary Anne let out a scream of horror.

'Go back!' she cried. 'Tell them you've changed your mind!'

'Too late,' James replied, grinning.

He didn't stop grinning all night. Finally, he was a soldier, just like he'd dreamed as a child.

He especially loved his sword. He had absolutely no intention of using it (nor the faintest idea how to do so) but he couldn't help but feel a shiver of pride every time he glanced down and caught sight of its gleaming blade at his thigh.

In fact, James was so taken with his uniform that he posed for a miniature portrait of himself to commemorate his commission, regularly taking it out of his pocket and gazing at it with wonder and pride, the ghost of Margaret by now long forgotten.

He knew he was taking a massive risk, bigger than ever before. In Edinburgh he'd had his own flat to retreat to every night. In the Army, privacy would be in short supply and he was going to have to be very careful indeed if he was to avoid

detection. Still, James was certain, it was a risk worth taking.

Unfortunately, the reality of being a soldier in the British Army was nowhere near as glamorous as James had envisaged. When he'd signed up, he'd pictured far-flung travel and endless adventure. The reality of life as a 'hospital assistant' (the first rung on the ladder to becoming a fully-fledged surgeon) was a lot less exciting.

His first posting was just a few miles away from his front door, at the York Hospital in nearby Chelsea.

It was miserable work. The hospital was dirty, crowded and noisy, the work bloody and relentless. Living conditions for the junior staff were notoriously bad. The food was terrible, the bedding was damp and dirty and, as a result of the filthy conditions, James and his colleagues suffered with regular sickness and diarrhoea.

However, there was one upside to the filth and chaos. Everyone was far too preoccupied to give much thought to James's small stature or unusually high voice, and he was free to go about his business unchallenged, honing his surgery skills along the way.

His hard work was rewarded and within a matter of months, he was given the position of acting assistant surgeon.

Despite the promotion, James remained desperate for a posting abroad and all the adventure it promised.

Unfortunately, although his official age was eighteen, some people still suspected that he was younger and the authorities refused to authorize it. As the weeks ticked by, James began to fear he'd be stuck in London for ever. Luckily, Buchan – who continued to follow James's progress with keen interest – came to the rescue, writing a firmly worded letter suggesting a more suitable posting be found.

Finally, after months of toiling away in Chelsea, a position was found for James at a military general hospital in Plymouth. It wasn't quite the exotic destination James had in mind but he wasn't exactly in a position to be picky.

On arrival in Plymouth, the Principal Medical Officer, a gentleman called Joseph Skey was visibly dismayed at James's youthful appearance.

'I'm sorry but there's no way I can have him on my staff,' he told the Board, fresh from meeting James for the first time. 'He's a mere child!'

James was horribly frustrated but as he had no way of proving his age, there was nothing he could do. Once again, it was up to Buchan to intervene on James's behalf, vouching not only for his age but also his supreme skill as a surgeon. Skey gave in, and even though James soon proved he was more than up to the job, people still refused to believe he could possibly be eighteen, deciding instead that he was a child prodigy of sixteen at the very, very most. Unwilling to risk drawing extra attention to himself by making a fuss or trying to prove otherwise, James had no choice but to play along with the whole silly charade.

Then, *finally*, in the summer of 1816, James's prayers were answered. He'd been given an overseas posting.

And *what* a posting!

After two long years of home service treading water in Chelsea, then Plymouth, he was bound for the Cape of Good Hope, situated in the Cape Colony at the most southern tip of Africa.

The Cape of Good Hope. The name alone filled James's heart with joy.

At last he was embarking on the kind of adventure he'd been dreaming of since he was a child.

CROSSING THE LINE

James watched in horror as one of his fellow passengers was dragged across the deck, kicking and shouting in protest.

The watching crowd meanwhile was delighted, laughing as a blindfold was fastened around the poor unsuspecting man's head. Next, he was hauled onto a plank over a large barrel of water where his face was smeared with a mixture of tar and grease.

'What are you doing?' he cried.

The crowd roared with laughter.

'You'll see,' one of the men carrying out the bizarre ritual replied. 'Now hold still.'

James watched as the sticky mixture on the man's face was shaved off and the plank was yanked away, leaving him to plunge into the filthy water.

The crowd whooped and applauded as the poor man hauled himself out of the barrel.

'Right,' the ringleader said, rubbing his hands together with glee. 'Who's next?'

One by one, all eligible men were forced to submit to the undignified ritual. They all went along with it, until one point-blank refused. However, it quickly became clear that sitting out was not an option. For daring to resist, the unfortunate man was held down and stripped naked, before being dunked in the murky water regardless.

'Anyone else?' the ringleader asked, his eyes scanning the deck for any final victims.

'What about him?' one of his cronies asked, pointing at James.

His heart thumping in his chest, James took a step backwards and shot a desperate look at the captain.

'Not him,' the captain said.

'Why not?' the ringleader asked.

The captain raised an eyebrow. 'Are you questioning my authority?' he asked.

'Of course not,' the ringleader stammered.

'Good.'

And with that, the ritual was over.

Relieved, James dashed back to his cabin before anyone could change their mind.

If James had learned anything over the last five years it was that research was vital. With that in mind,

he'd spent the weeks leading up to his departure for the Cape by meticulously researching every aspect of the journey. Faced with the prospect of three whole months with next to no privacy, James didn't want to get on board to find any nasty surprises.

He quickly ascertained that the ship he would be travelling on, the *Lord Cathcart* was *not* designed for comfort. It was primarily a merchant vessel, with the likes of James shoved into cramped shared cabins on the gun deck. One small perk he discovered was that as an officer he would at least have access to a private privy, ensuring he could at least use the toilet undisturbed (a small but not insignificant comfort).

It was during his research process that he came across the 'Crossing the Line' ritual. Any passenger who was crossing the Equator for the first time would be subjected to it.

Women were spared the treatment, but, of course, James could not use the gender he'd been assigned at birth to avoid the ordeal.

Horrified, James had boarded the ship knowing that he had to get out of the ritual, no matter what it took. He made sure to talk to the captain immediately, presented him with a gallon of rum and a couple of pounds of sugar and hoped for the best. Now, as James lay down on his bunk, he thanked his lucky stars that he'd done his homework properly.

The rest of the voyage passed more or less peacefully and gave James a much-needed confidence boost. Yes, his appearance remained slightly unconventional, but arriving at the Cape, his good reputation still intact, he felt ready for whatever this strange new world might throw at him.

The first thing James noticed was the heat. Back in England it was autumn, the leaves would be falling and the cold weather would be setting in by now, but here in the Cape, summer was just beginning, the vegetation lush and green and the days long and sultry. Compared to the dirty grey streets of London, the scenery was like something out of a dream – mountains in one direction, azure blue seas in the other.

James was captivated.

He reported for duty with the Chief Medical Officer before setting about finding somewhere to live. He soon identified a comfortable set of rooms in a lodging house near the botanical gardens that would fit the bill nicely. After the cramped conditions on board the ship, it was blissful to finally have a bit of comfort and privacy.

His next task was to befriend the Governor of the Cape, a gentleman by the name of Lord Somerset and the most powerful man in the colony. Feeling secure in his male persona after the successful voyage, James finally felt ready to make friends. With this in mind, he paid a visit to Somerset's home, armed with a letter of recommendation from good old Buchan.

A housekeeper answered the door and told James that Somerset was tied up at present, attending to his daughter Georgiana, who was very unwell.

'I'm a doctor,' James explained. 'Perhaps *I* could examine her?'

'Over ten different doctors have tried to help Miss Georgiana and not one of them has succeeded,' the housekeeper sniffed. 'I doubt you'll have any more luck.'

'It's surely worth a try,' James said.

'I'll ask the master. But don't count your chickens. What did you say your name was again?'

'Barry. Dr James Barry.'

A few minutes later Somerset emerged. He was a tall, striking man, but clearly in some distress, his handsome face lined with worry.

James extended his hand. 'Lord Somerset, it's an honour to meet you. Please accept this letter of recommendation from my good friend, the Earl of Buchan.'

At the mention of Buchan's name, Somerset brightened a little.

'Remind me of your name,' he said.

'Dr James Barry.'

Somerset snapped his fingers. 'Of course!' he cried. 'The child prodigy!'

James couldn't help but wince. Clearly his reputation (however inaccurate) preceded him.

'Do you really think you might help my daughter?' Somerset asked.

James puffed out his chest. 'I'll certainly do my best, my lord.'

Somerset led James up to Georgiana's bedroom. 'She's been ill for months now,' he explained. 'My wife died just two short years ago. I'm not sure I'll survive if I lose my dear sweet Georgiana too.'

'I will do everything within my power to stop that from happening,' James said.

He sat down beside Georgiana, taking her hand and introducing himself. Georgiana, who had been poked and prodded by every doctor in Cape Town, was immediately struck by James's gentle manner. Following a long chat and a physical examination, it was soon clear (to James, at least) that there was no physical reason for Georgiana's illness. In his opinion, it was a combination of homesickness and grief that was making her ill, and what she needed most was a kindly, sympathetic presence at her side. With this in mind he employed his very best bedside manner, attending to Georgiana day and night. Georgiana took to her new doctor straightaway, and James too became fond of his newest patient. After many years in a series of all-male environments, Georgiana's company made a pleasant change, and James soon discovered he might just have a knack for winning the trust of his female patients. Indeed, his approach worked, for within a few days Georgiana's condition was much improved and she eventually made a full recovery.

Somerset was delighted.

'Buchan was right!' he said, slapping James on the back. 'You really are a genius!'

And with that, James was welcomed into the Somerset family with open arms.

It was a pretty decent start.

James had only been in the Cape for a few weeks and he was already a hero.

A GRAND TOUR

Over the coming weeks, James's friendship with Somerset deepened. James could be incredibly charming when he wanted to be, and Somerset, still in mourning for his wife, was delighted by the witty new addition to Cape society. He was equally popular with Georgiana and Somerset's other daughter, Charlotte, and became a regular fixture at the Somersets' dinner table.

James was thrilled. After all those years of hiding away while studying at Edinburgh and keeping himself to himself in the barracks, he finally felt confident enough to socialize. Occasionally, he worried that his new friends might guess his secret, but so far they'd shown no indication they suspected anything was amiss, treating him more like one of the family than a guest.

In early 1817, Somerset embarked on a grand tour of the Cape Colony, and insisted that James join the party. James was hugely flattered, aware that his inclusion almost certainly cemented his position in Cape society.

The purpose of the tour was to survey the land with a view to encouraging British farmers to move to the area. James, thirsty for adventure and honoured by the invitation, agreed immediately.

The travelling party set out in late January. They left behind the town and ventured towards the mountains with little idea of exactly what lay ahead of them.

The roads quickly became too rough and bumpy to travel by carriage so they switched to horseback, their belongings and equipment carried on sturdy wagons.

The journey was a punishing one. It was incredibly hot, and early on they were faced with the prospect of tackling the Hottentots Holland Mountains, a stretch of forbidding peaks that separated the town and its surrounding area from the rest of the colony. There was only one possible route through and it was not an easy one. At times the path was dangerously steep and narrow. James, an inexperienced horseman at the best of times, feared for his life as they navigated the perilous route. An animal-lover, he winced every time he thwacked his horse, but the discipline was necessary – just one stumble and they might fall.

'Perhaps I should ride in one of the wagons?' he suggested as the path narrowed even further.

Seconds later, one of the oxen pulling the wagon up ahead of him, exhausted and dehydrated from the journey, slipped over the edge and fell down the steep mountainside, pulling the entire vehicle and everything on board with it.

'Perhaps not,' James murmured, resisting the urge to look down.

Miraculously, James somehow managed to stay on his horse and the party emerged on the other side of the mountain more or less in one piece.

The hardest bit of the journey out of the way, James could finally relax a little and take in the breath-taking surroundings. He was particularly taken by the abundance of plants and their medicinal properties, studying them with excitement. There was wildlife everywhere he looked and James was thrilled to be able to observe rare species like the bontebok (a species of antelope with beautiful chocolate-coloured fur) and the hippopotamus, as well as monkeys, elephants, lizards, and parrots with feathers all the colours of the rainbow.

'It's like stepping into the pages of a storybook,' he said in wonder, much to the delight of his far more worldly companions.

Although there were women on the tour (namely Georgiana and Charlotte Somerset), James knew there was no way he'd have had the opportunity to see such wonders if he'd remained living as Margaret. Every single day he felt grateful he wasn't cooped up in some dreary London house, earning a pittance working as a governess or companion.

In the evenings, James and Somerset regularly stayed up late, talking around the fire. They discussed everything from art and literature, to science and nature, as well as more personal subjects like Somerset's wife's death and his enduring love for his daughters. These conversations were a revelation for James. Apart from his mother (who he didn't really count), he hadn't had a truly meaningful conversation with another human being since the days of Fryer and Miranda. Although he knew there was no way he could risk truly opening up to Somerset, he felt like he'd finally forged a genuine friendship.

One night, a few weeks in to their journey, the group set up camp as usual. As night fell, James retreated to his tent and drifted off to sleep. A few hours later, he awoke to a blood-curdling scream. He was scrambling to make himself decent when he heard footsteps approaching the tent.

'Dr Barry!' a voice called. 'Are you awake? You're needed!'

'Stay back!' James yelped. 'I'll be out in a moment!'

As soon as he was satisfied that he was presentable, James ventured out of the tent to see what was going on.

A boy who by day worked on the wagons had been asleep under the stars when a curious lion slipped past the camp guards, grabbed the poor boy in its hungry mouth and dragged him off towards the trees. The guards immediately gave chase, yelling and screaming. Their shouts startled the lion, prompting it to drop the boy before retreating into the trees.

The guards carried the poor boy back to the camp where James was waiting.

'Give us room,' James ordered.

The party obeyed, scattering immediately.

James rolled up his sleeves and examined the boy. Quite incredibly, apart from a few scratches and bite marks, he wasn't seriously hurt. He was more shocked than anything, his eyes wide with fright from his ordeal. With his trademark efficiency and care, James treated the boy's wounds and calmed him down.

'Aren't we lucky you were here!' Georgiana said admiringly.

'James to the rescue yet again,' Charlotte chimed in.

James basked in their praise, delighted that he'd proved himself to be so very useful.

Gradually, everyone drifted back to their tents and went back to sleep, the excitement over.

Everyone apart from James.

He lay wide awake for hours, a huge grin on his face. Who cared that they could have all been mauled to death by a lion? He'd been craving adventure his entire life and now here he was – slap bang in the middle of one.

Several weeks into the trip, the group stopped to rest at the home of an English landowner called George Rex. Famously hospitable, Rex was delighted to have visitors to his remote estate, laying on fishing trips and shooting parties, as well as rowdy social gatherings every evening.

James enjoyed his stay hugely. Despite his years of refusing invitations in Edinburgh, he was a naturally social creature.

He particularly relished the opportunity to bond with Rex's many offspring. Although he had never wanted to become a governess, James had always enjoyed the company of children and Rex's large brood was no exception. The children were lively and affectionate and took to James immediately, following him everywhere he went. A couple of the older children noted the kapok (a kind of plant fibre) stuffing in the lining of James's clothing. This led to a rather unfortunate nickname – *Kapok Nooientjie* (or Little Kapok Maiden). The nickname soon took off, with many of Rex's staff using it to refer to their slightly unusual guest. Although the rest of the tour party didn't seem to get wind of it, it was a stark reminder that no matter how secure his position in society, James couldn't let anyone get too close to him, no matter how tempting.

A BEDSIDE VIGIL

Back in Cape Town, James's star continued to rise. Thanks to his ongoing association with Somerset, more and more citizens began to seek out his services. In addition to his work at the military hospital, James became extremely busy with private work. However, he refused to take payment from any of his private patients, insisting they cover his expenses and nothing more. Although his Army salary was not large, it was more than enough for him to live comfortably and he disapproved of other doctors who boasted of lining their pockets with fees from private patients.

James soon became famous both for his excellent bedside manner *and* for his terrible temper. Gentle and nurturing with his patients, James had absolutely no time for incompetent nurses or pompous doctors and would regularly fly off the handle if his instructions were not followed to the letter. Such a fiery reputation only served to increase James's fame and popularity with patients. Quite often, dazzled by James's success rate, they presented him with gifts instead, many of which he *did* accept. When his treatment resulted in the full recovery of a woman thought to be close to death from pneumonia, James was gifted with two beautiful black horses, as well as regular deliveries of food for them. On another occasion he was presented with a diamond ring! Despite being surrounded by such wealth, James never forgot his vow to help those less fortunate. He ensured his door was always open to anyone who needed his help.

Somerset's friendship also meant that James had quickly been elevated into Cape society. His life was full and rewarding. He worked hard but he also played hard, balancing his medical duties with countless parties and social events. He was a good dancer and an excellent flirt, winning countless hearts and earning himself the reputation as a bit of a 'ladies' man'. After so many years of hiding himself away, James was in his element and wrote a series of enthusiastic letters to his mother back in London, describing his exciting new life in the sunshine.

*   *   *

Then, in October 1818, disaster struck. Somerset fell gravely ill. James rushed to his bedside and was dismayed to find his dear friend weak and feverish. James examined him and diagnosed him with typhus and dysentery. Three other doctors, all much more senior than James, arrived on the scene and declared Somerset's situation hopeless and any efforts to cure him a waste of time and energy. They were so certain of his imminent death they even gave orders that the colonial ship *Mary* should be prepared to dispatch bad news back to London.

James was furious. 'I know he's ill,' he roared. 'But that doesn't mean we should just give up!'

The men argued back and forth, before finally agreeing that James should take sole responsibility for Somerset's care.

James hid it well, but he was out of his depth. He had little experience of treating either typhus *or* dysentery, with most of his knowledge coming from the pages of textbooks. However, he was determined not to let Somerset down. After all, he was James's closest friend, and without him James's position in the Cape would be nowhere near as secure. All the connections James had made up to this point were down to Somerset. He was not stupid. Just like during his days in Edinburgh, he was aware of the whispers about his odd appearance and unusual mannerisms. His association with the powerful and respected Somerset meant the gossip went no further.

James tried every kind of treatment he could think of. Unwilling to trust anyone else to administer his strict instructions, James did everything himself, from collecting Somerset's stools for inspection, to bathing him. He was so dedicated he barely slept for days on end, keeping a permanent vigil at Somerset's bedside. As he watched over his friend, it dawned on James just how fragile his position was. He may have been the Cape's most in-demand doctor, but without Somerset as his protector, who knew what would become of him?

Eventually though, his efforts began to pay off. Somerset rallied. Much to everyone's extreme surprise, within just a few weeks, he was back to his usual self, merrily dictating letters, and making plans for the coming months.

Dr James Barry, the boy wonder, had done it again!

As a result, Somerset was even more in awe of James's skill than ever, declaring James a genius to everyone who would listen. Moreover, the scare brought the two men closer than ever before. Inevitably, though, their relationship attracted criticism. Some thought it inappropriate for Somerset, as Governor, to exhibit such blatant favouritism, while others were flat-out jealous that

James had wormed his way into the most important household in the Cape with such speed and apparent ease. James didn't care. He adored his friend, and knew that as long as they remained close, his role in Cape society was safe (along with his secret).

Shortly after Somerset's miraculous recovery, James's position as personal physician to the Governor and his household was formalized and he was presented with a dog as a token of Somerset's gratitude – a small white poodle James named Psyche.

But Somerset's friendship couldn't keep him safe for ever.

A DANGEROUS MISTAKE

By 1819, James had been living as a man for almost ten years. Although he still cut a slightly unconventional figure, he no longer spent every waking moment worried he was about to be found out.

However, danger still lurked around every corner. As James discovered late one spring night…

James often worked alongside an English nurse named Sarah. James didn't like many nurses but he liked this one. Sarah was highly trained and efficient and responded well to his very specific instructions.

One of their cases involved them both staying overnight at the family home of a female patient.

Sarah was on duty when she realized the woman they were treating needed urgent medical attention.

Quickly, she sent for James. When he did not emerge from his quarters, she decided to run to fetch him herself. As it was an emergency, she didn't bother to knock, bursting into the room unannounced to discover James in his undergarments.

Upon seeing him in a state of undress, she let out a gasp.

'Get out!' James screamed at her. 'Now!'

Sarah apologized and ran from the room in shock.

On the other side of the door, James's hands shook. Sarah had seen his female body, that much was clear. But what would happen now? Would she tell? And if she did, what would the consequences be? James couldn't even bring himself to imagine.

For the next few days, he kept a low profile, jumping out of his skin every time there was a knock at the door. A week passed and James felt confident that Sarah hadn't blabbed. Still, he remained cautious. Just because Sarah hadn't revealed his secret yet, it didn't mean she wouldn't at some point in the future. To be safe, he made sure he never worked with her again, and if their paths did cross, he made a point of ignoring her. A few months later, Sarah left the Cape for good, taking James's secret with her.

Following this incident, James's old insecurities resurfaced. He became increasingly stressed, and his reputation for shouting, slamming doors and flying off the handle at the slightest thing only grew. Even

Somerset wasn't immune. If he didn't follow James's medical instructions to the letter, James would scold him quite thoroughly.

It was perhaps this heightened state of stress that led to James making a huge mistake – one with almost fatal consequences.

Captain Josias Cloete was a seasoned war veteran who had recently returned to the Cape from action in India. James decided he disliked Cloete before he'd even met him, having heard on the grapevine that Cloete was also favoured by Somerset. Upon meeting, it soon became clear that the feeling was mutual, despite the fact both men had lots in common. In addition to their individual friendships with Somerset, they were both hugely ambitious and were well known for their prickliness. Perhaps most oddly of all, they also resembled each other physically, from hair and eye colour, to strikingly similar features (large wide eyes, long, curved noses and full lips). On his return to the Cape, Cloete saw that James and Somerset had grown close, and became horribly jealous. James also felt threatened by the new arrival and had no intention of sharing Somerset with Cloete. From the beginning, they were hostile to each other.

One evening James, keen to at least try and make conversation with his rival, made a crude comment about a lady who was visiting Somerset.

This was a terrible error. It was simply unacceptable for an officer to comment on a lady's appearance to another officer and Cloete was not happy.

'What did you say?' Cloete asked.

James, still unaware of the seriousness of his misstep, repeated his quip.

'Retract it immediately!' Cloete cried, unable to conceal his anger.

James, although he'd realized his mistake by this point, refused out of pure stubbornness. Cloete, by now in a terrible rage, made his anger known by pulling on James's nose. Unwilling to start brawling (unbecoming behaviour for two men of their class), James made an incredibly bold move.

He challenged Cloete to a duel in order to decide the matter!

'A duel?' Cloete repeated.

'Yes,' James said.

'Fine,' Cloete said, storming out of the room.

James remained in his seat, trembling violently. What on earth had he done? Cloete was a trained soldier, and a highly decorated one at that. James may have worn an Army uniform but he'd had next to no military training. This was not to mention the fact that being killed or wounded ramped up the risk of his biological sex being discovered. Despite this, there was no question of pulling out. He was a gentleman, and gentlemen stuck to their word, no matter how dire the consequences.

The necessary arrangements were made, and a few days later James found himself rising before dawn, dressing in full Army uniform and travelling by coach to the chosen location for the duel – the beach.

Somerset had no idea the duel was taking place. James and Cloete had both agreed it was better he not find out.

As the coach rattled through the silent streets, James stroked his dog Psyche's ears and tried not to panic.

On arrival, Cloete was waiting. He was not alone. As per tradition, a number of witnesses had been assembled.

James and Cloete were each given an opportunity to offer an apology or retraction. This was James's last chance to pull out.

He didn't take it.

Their pistols were loaded. James was not used to handling firearms of any kind and his gun felt alien in his hand – heavy and unwieldy.

The rules of the duel were very strict. Once combat had begun, it must continue, shot after shot, until at least one of the men was either wounded or dead. No matter what the outcome, blood would be shed, and it would probably be James's. Even worse than that, though, was the prospect of his dead or unconscious body being examined and him being absolutely unable to do anything to stop it.

James knelt down and spoke sternly to Psyche, warning him to keep his distance.

A surgeon was on hand to tend to any wounds. As James strode the ten paces to his marker point, he noticed the man opening his case and laying out his equipment, making ready.

James swallowed hard and turned to face Cloete. The sun was beginning to come up, making the waves sparkle. If he weren't quite so terrified, he would have probably found the scene rather beautiful.

His heart was beating so loudly it was deafening. He exhaled long and slow in an attempt to steady his shallow breathing and put his finger on the trigger.

The waving of a white handkerchief signalled the start of the duel. Before James even had the chance to think, he pulled the trigger. Cloete did the same. Against all the odds, James's aim was the better of the two, his bullet clipping the peak of Cloete's hat. He had no time to feel triumphant, for at that precise moment he became aware of an excruciating pain in his leg.

He looked down. His trousers were covered in blood. Cloete's shot had hit him on the upper thigh, dangerously close to his groin. Out of the corner of his eye, James could see the surgeon rushing towards him, scissors in hand. James had to act fast for he knew exactly what the scissors were for. They were to cut away James's trousers so the surgeon could attend to his wound more quickly.

'Stay back!' James yelled.

Startled, the surgeon stopped in his tracks. 'But you're bleeding,' he protested.

'I'm a doctor,' James said. 'I'll take care of it. Now, if you'll excuse me.'

As the surgeon, Cloete and the small group of witnesses watched in utter astonishment, James turned away and bound the wound himself.

'Are you sure you're all right?' Cloete asked as the two men shook hands (as was customary following a duel).

'Perfectly,' James said through gritted teeth. He bid the group goodbye and staggered back towards his carriage, ignoring the surgeon's continued pleas to allow him to treat the wound properly.

Back at home and in quite some pain, James shut the door behind him and yanked off his bloodied breeches. Thankfully, it was just a flesh wound and needed only to be cleaned and bandaged. James knew how fortunate he'd been. The bullet could have hit an artery, resulting in almost certain death. Perhaps more terrifyingly, if the bullet had gone in even just a tiny bit deeper than it had, immediate surgery would have been needed and James's secret would have been out.

He had been extraordinarily lucky.

MAKING A DIFFERENCE

As it turned out, James's escapade actually had several unexpectedly positive consequences. Firstly, his adherence to the rules of duelling confirmed his status as a gentleman. Secondly, his fearsome reputation was stronger than ever. At the same time, it was a powerful reminder that James couldn't get complacent – not now, not ever.

His popularity soared and he found himself on the guest list of every society party in town. Although he enjoyed them hugely, the fancy dinners and balls only served to remind him of the huge gap between the rich and the poor. He'd never forgotten the poverty he witnessed back in London, and the more powerful and respected he became, the more determined he was to use his knowledge and status to help others less fortunate than him. The Cape may have been sunny, but many of its people led lives that were anything but and James was desperate to change this in any way he could.

James was especially horrified by the treatment of slaves on the Cape, and the lack of respect for the indigenous people who had been living there for centuries before the Dutch and, later, the British turned up and took over. The plight of one particular young boy caught James's attention.

Known as Hermes, the boy was kept by a Dutch woman who was unspeakably cruel to him, beating him regularly and depriving him of food and water. Starving and desperate, one night he stole some food from her kitchen. The woman caught him and was threatening to have him thrown in the prison when James heard of his struggle and intervened. He bought Hermes's freedom and found a new home for the boy with a kindly family who welcomed him into the fold and treated him with the kindness and respect he deserved.

Individual acts of charity were all well and good but James knew that in order to make a real difference, he needed to act on a much bigger scale. And in early 1822, he was given the power to do just that.

In March, the Cape's Colonial Medical Inspector, a gentleman called Dr John Robb, resigned unexpectedly. In need of a replacement, Somerset gave James the job. His appointment shocked many of the Cape's residents. Although well known for his expertise as a doctor, James was still only a lowly assistant staff surgeon. His new role represented a huge promotion and fresh whispers of favouritism spread like wildfire.

James didn't care what people were saying. His appointment gave him authority over every medical practitioner in the Cape. It also made him responsible for (amongst many other things) prisons, civilian hospitals, sanitation and the treatment of the clinically insane and the poor... Finally, he could make a real difference to people's lives on a large scale.

One of his first tasks was to consult on the case of a young slave who had been beaten to death by his master. The autopsy confirmed that he had been killed, but the family of the murderer had ordered their own autopsy, which claimed the body showed no evidence of beating. James immediately dismissed the second autopsy and forbade it from being used in court. The murderer was promptly found guilty and sentenced to death, while the doctor who conducted the second autopsy was struck off the register for incompetence and corruption.

It was clear to everyone in the Cape that James meant business.

Next on his list were the apothecaries. It had come to his attention that they were poorly regulated and many were illegally selling medicines that contained dangerous amounts of ingredients like arsenic, mercury and lead. Within a few short months, measures were brought in to stop such practices, with hefty punishments put in place for those who defied James's new rules.

However, James's main priority remained as improving conditions for the most vulnerable members of society. He had become aware of the plight of leprosy sufferers back in 1817 when he'd toured the Cape with Somerset, and now he had the power, he was determined to do something to improve their lives.

Leprosy, also known as Hansen's disease, is a long-term infection that causes damage to the respiratory tract, nerves, eyes and skin. In the 1800s it was still hugely misunderstood with sufferers in some parts of the world (including the Cape) segregated from the rest of the population and placed in institutes.

The Cape's Leper Institution wasn't officially on his list of responsibilities, but James requested Somerset add supervision of it to his already groaning workload. Somerset reluctantly agreed and James set off for the Institute to see what kind of conditions the patients were living in.

He'd feared the worst – but even that couldn't prepare him for the horrors that greeted him.

The Institute was filthy and crowded with not enough bed linen for the 150 inmates, never mind proper beds. James spoke to the diseased inmates about their living conditions and asked them to share their complaints.

'We're constantly hungry,' one explained.

'We're forced to labour in the garden,' another said.

'And if we're unable to do so, we're punished,' someone else chipped in.

'In what way?' James asked.

'They take away our food. Or don't let us go outside.'

'That's if you're lucky,' another man said, showing James the unmistakable marks of a recent flogging on his back.

'It's surely better to die of disease rather than cruelty and hunger,' another remarked.

James was furious. These people needed care, not punishment.

He sacked all the staff on the spot and set about completely reorganizing the Institute. Over the coming months he made the 150-mile round trip from Cape Town to the Institution several times to check that his instructions were being followed. His dedication paid off and conditions improved hugely under his watchful eye.

Over the next few years, James swept through the Cape's prisons and hospitals, asylums and apothecaries, stamping out corruption and putting new systems in place. He enjoyed great success and improved the lives of thousands of vulnerable people – but he also made a great many enemies along the way. Many government officials did not like being told what to do, and James became deeply unpopular with some of the most powerful men in the Cape. James knew this but didn't care. He wasn't afraid of them and he certainly wasn't going to let them prevent him doing his job properly. James continued to put the needs of the poor and disadvantaged first, unaware that a plot to get rid of him was brewing.

TOO BIG FOR HIS BOOTS

One deceptively ordinary morning in August 1825, James received a request from David Denyssen, the government official in charge of the Cape's prisons. He wanted James to authorize the transfer of a prisoner by the name of Aaron Smith to the lunatic asylum at the hospital.

It quickly became clear the case wasn't as straightforward as Denyssen made it out to be. Smith was a sailor who had been detained at the prison following a drunken binge during which he had trashed Denyssen's property. Under strict instructions from Denyssen, a local doctor had certified Smith as 'deranged in his mind' and recommended for him to be confined to the lunatic asylum indefinitely.

James had already had a number of run-ins with Denyssen. James thought Denyssen was a bully who enabled – and on some occasions even encouraged – the ill-treatment of his prisoners. Denyssen thought James was a meddling busybody who was getting far too big for his boots.

James took one look at the Smith file and immediately deduced that Denyssen was punishing Smith for attacking his property. Fed up with Denyssen's cruel and self-serving behaviour, James wrote his report, making it clear he knew exactly what Denyssen was up to and that he wasn't impressed. He knew it would ruffle a few feathers but he wasn't too worried, certain that Somerset would back him up if needed.

Upon reading the report, Denyssen was predictably furious. It was a public document that anyone could read if they so wished and he was incandescent with rage that James had cast him in such a poor light.

'How dare he speak about me like that?' he roared to anyone who would listen.

Instead of shaming him into releasing Smith, the report had the exact opposite effect. Denyssen ignored James's recommendation that Smith be allowed to go free, leaving him to languish in prison instead!

'And if Barry doesn't like it,' he cackled, 'he can lump it!'

Upon learning of Denyssen's decision, a furious James went to visit Smith in prison. He was horrified to discover him ill and dangerously weak, his body scrawny from the lack of food, his bony back scarred from regular beatings at the hands of the prison guards. Trembling with anger, James went home and wrote a second report, detailing Smith's plight at the hands of the self-serving Denyssen. Little did he know he was playing right into Denyssen's hands...

James had almost finished when he heard a knock at the door.

A messenger was on the doorstep with a summons for James to appear before a commission of the Court of Justice.

'On what grounds?' James demanded.

'You're required to defend your criticism of the prisons department,' the messenger replied nervously.

Immediately, James knew Denyssen was behind the summons. Furious, he ripped it up there and then, throwing the bits of paper in the poor messenger's face. He was so angry and upset he even threatened to cut off Denyssen's ear 'with a sword'.

Once he'd calmed down, he realized there was nothing he could do to avoid a formal court summons, no matter how unjust, and so when a second arrived the following day, he did not rip it up, and reluctantly attended as requested.

However, James had no intention of acknowledging the 'ridiculous' claims made against him. Indeed, he refused to utter a word, hoping his silence would make it clear he thought the entire process was a sham.

Unfortunately, his plan backfired. Denyssen was not the only one fed up with James, and the court took Denyssen's side. James was sentenced to civil imprisonment unless he withdrew his criticisms of Denyssen. The idea of publicly excusing Denyssen made James feel sick, but the possible consequences if he refused were just too great. With a heavy heart, James agreed to withdraw his comments and his original report, hoping it would mark the end of the entire mess.

Sadly, it was just the beginning.

Unbeknownst to James, the plot against him was building and Denyssen was by no means the only person involved. Another senior official (and close friend of Denyssen), a man by the name of William Plaskett had been busy. While James had been stuck in court, he'd complied a dossier of complaints about James's various dealings across the Cape and come to the conclusion that James had been given far too much power for someone of his standing, and that Somerset was squarely to blame.

Desperate for support, James turned to Somerset, certain his protector would be able to put a stop to the nonsense at once. Sadly, on this occasion there was nothing the Governor could do. The truth was, although James was more than up to the job of Colonial Medical Inspector, he would never have been given the role were it not for his friendship with Somerset. Until now, his critics had broadly kept their feelings on the matter to themselves, but suddenly the floodgates were open and a number of Cape officials were calling on Somerset to formally withdraw his support for James.

'I'm sorry, James,' Somerset said. 'But there's nothing I can do. I'm being accused of professional misconduct. If I publicly support you on this matter, I'll be putting my entire reputation at risk.'

The realization that even someone as powerful and respected as Somerset couldn't help him was a terrible blow. With no one else to turn to, James had no choice but to leave the contents of the damning report unchallenged.

A few days later it was announced that the role of Chief Medical Inspector would cease to exist with immediate effect. Instead, a medical board would be appointed in its place, on which James could serve as a junior member if he so wished. It was a bitter blow. James was devastated at the prospect of having the job he adored torn from beneath his feet.

'A junior member?' James cried when Somerset told him of the offer. 'I'd rather you just sacked me altogether!'

'I'm sorry,' Somerset said. 'But my hands are tied. This is the very best I can offer right now.'

'Pah!' James replied.

Somerset begged him to take the role but James refused.

'I'm sorry, but I can't. It's just too humiliating.'

And so, after nine years in the Cape, James found himself exactly where he had started – as a lowly assistant surgeon earning seven shillings and sixpence per day – a pittance compared to the salary he'd enjoyed as Chief Medical Inspector.

And things were about to get even worse. As a result of all the drama, Somerset had been summoned back to England to defend his own behaviour in the whole saga. James had hoped he might be invited along as Somerset's personal physician but it was not to be. Somerset had clearly decided to distance himself from his friend, not even mentioning the possibility of James joining him in England, a move that James found deeply hurtful.

On a chilly March day in 1826, the entire Somerset family sailed away, leaving James behind – alone and disgraced. Within the space of just a few months, he'd lost both the job he loved and his best friend and protector. For the first time since getting off the *Lord Cathcart* nearly a decade earlier, he questioned whether he should have just followed his mother's advice and chosen the quiet life as a countryside doctor. It would have been boring, but surely intense boredom was preferable over the pain and loss he was feeling watching his dearest friend sail away, possibly never to return. As Somerset's ship disappeared beyond the horizon, a tear trickled down James's cheek and he doubted he'd ever felt so wretched in his entire life.

MAKING HISTORY

Following Somerset's departure, James hit rock bottom. He'd lost everything – his protector, his position, his place in society – and no matter how hard he tried, he couldn't see a way of getting any of them back. His life, once lively and exciting, was now desperately quiet and lonely. James was still in demand as a doctor, but the invitations to the parties and balls and shooting expeditions that once poured through his letterbox on an almost daily basis had all but dried up. News of the nasty business with Denyssen had spread, and as a result James had earned the reputation for being a troublemaker. With no Somerset to smooth things over, James had no choice but to keep his head down and hope the rumours would die out eventually.

This all changed late one wet and windy July night in 1826.

Somerset had been gone for several months at this point, and James was still an outcast. Instead of time healing his pain, he felt more miserable than ever. At night, he lay in bed torturing himself over the choices he'd made and the path he'd taken. He went over every single decision, desperately trying to work out what the outcome might have been if he'd been a little less selfish, a little more sensible.

He was agonizing in this fashion when he heard a loud hammering at the front door shortly after 2 a.m. James heaved himself out of bed, pulling on his dressing gown and a pair of slippers. He was not unduly concerned by the urgent knocking – he was used to being woken up in the night to attend to medical emergencies.

He opened the door to reveal a young boy standing on the doorstep. He was out of breath, his pale face streaked with rain.

'Come quickly,' the boy panted. 'You're needed at the Munnik household right away.'

James recognized the name immediately. The Munniks were one of the Cape's richest and most respected families.

'Why? What's happened?' he asked.

'The lady of the house is in childbirth but something isn't right. Please, come quickly.'

'Let me get my things,' James said, before bounding up the stairs to dress and collect his doctor's bag.

A few minutes later, he was in a carriage bound for the Munnik family home, a sprawling mansion on the edge of town. Although James had delivered several babies over the course of his career, the job was usually left to the midwives. Doctors were generally only called if the baby was in distress.

He arrived to discover Mr Munnik and his sister-in-law waiting anxiously at the door. There was no time for formal introductions with Munnik pouncing on James the moment he reached them.

'It's my wife,' Mr Munnik said, his voice trembling and his eyes wild with fear. 'Wilhelmina.'

'Take me to her at once,' James said.

They headed upstairs to the master bedroom where Wilhelmina was lying in bed. She was obviously in some distress, sweat and tears running down her exhausted face.

'What's going on?' James barked at the midwife.

She explained that Wilhelmina had been in labour for over twenty-four hours but the baby was yet to be born and Wilhelmina was losing strength by the minute.

'I've never had a labour go on so long,' the midwife confided. 'If we don't do something soon, we're going to lose them both, I know it!'

James ordered everyone out of the way and sat down beside Wilhelmina.

'I'm James,' he said, taking care to make his voice as calm and gentle as possible. 'I'm going to deliver your baby for you.'

He examined Wilhelmina. The baby had a heartbeat but it was fading quickly. If he did not get a move on, both mother and baby would be in grave danger, just as the midwife feared.

It was time to make a decision – one with life-or-death consequences.

He took the midwife aside.

'I believe there's only one course of action,' he said in a whisper.

'Yes?' the midwife asked, wringing her hands.

'We're going to have to perform a Caesarean section.'

The midwife let out a gasp. 'You can't be serious?' she said.

'We have no choice,' James replied.

'What's going on?' Mr Munnik asked, joining them.

'Dr Barry wants to attempt a Caesarean section,' the midwife hissed.

'A Caesarean what?' Mr Munnik said.

'It's an operation,' James explained. 'I'll make an incision in Wilhelmina's abdomen and deliver the baby that way.'

'Over my dead body!' Mr Munnik cried.

'Excuse me for speaking out of turn, Mr Munnik,' James said. 'But it will be Wilhelmina's dead body if we don't at least give it a try.'

'But it's never been done before!' the midwife squeaked.

'That's not true,' James replied. 'I admit it's a rare procedure, but there have been at least six recorded attempts.'

He chose not to add that in at least half of these cases, either the mother or child had lost their lives.

'These successful attempts you speak of,' Mr Munnik said. 'Were you personally responsible for any of them?'

'No,' James admitted.

'But you were in the room?'

'Not exactly.'

'Hold on a moment, are you seriously telling me you're proposing to perform an operation on my wife you've never even seen done before?'

'That's right.'

'But how will you even know what to do?'

James hesitated. The truth was, the closest he'd got to performing the procedure was reading an account in a textbook.

'But that's preposterous!' Mr Munnik cried when James admitted this.

'That may be so,' James said. 'But right now we have very little choice. If we do nothing, Wilhelmina and your unborn child will almost certainly die. If I attempt the procedure, they at least have a chance of survival.' *However small*, he secretly thought.

'What's going on?' Wilhelmina cried from her bed. 'What are you all talking about?'

'Nothing, darling,' Mr Munnik said.

'I don't believe you,' Wilhelmina wailed. 'Tell me at once.'

James sat down beside her and outlined his plan and the risks involved, with Mr Munnik glowering behind him all the while.

'You don't have to go along with this,' Mr Munnik said. 'We can call another doctor, get a second opinion.'

'No,' Wilhelmina said, her voice now firm despite the immense pain she was in. 'I want to do it.'

'Is this really our only chance to save them both?' Mr Munnik asked James.

'Yes,' James replied.

'Please,' Wilhelmina said, clutching at her bed sheets in pain. 'Anything to save my baby!'

Mr Munnik turned to James. 'Do what you need to do.'

Immediately, James got to work, barking orders at the midwife and servants, before sitting at Wilhelmina's side and calmly explaining exactly what the procedure involved. Inside, he felt anything but calm, his mind racing a million miles per hour as he tried to picture the diagrams in the textbook.

With no nurses at his disposal, James had to rely on the midwife and two house servants to assist him. It wasn't ideal (the two servants were just teenagers and from what James could gather had no medical training whatsoever) but he had little choice in the matter.

James cast his gaze around the opulently decorated bedroom.

'We need to move her,' he said. Items like bed linen and curtains carried infection and he needed the patient to be lying on a flat, firm surface. He proposed relocating to the kitchen.

With some difficulty, everyone worked together to carry poor Wilhelmina down to the kitchen where she was laid out on the hastily cleared table.

There would be no pain relief. This was 1826, several years before anaesthesia became available. Instead, the two servants held Wilhelmina down (one by her shoulders, the other by her ankles) while Wilhelmina herself was given a leather strap to bite on.

'I'm scared,' she said, frightened tears running down her face.

James took her hands in his and looked deep into her eyes. 'I know you are,' he replied. 'But it will all be over soon, I promise.'

He longed to tell her that everything would be all right, but he simply couldn't bring himself to tell lies. Despite his calm exterior he was terrified at the enormity of what he was about to attempt.

He reached for his scalpel and surveyed Wilhelmina's swollen belly.

'I'm going to start the procedure now, Wilhelmina,' he said.

Wilhelmina nodded, closed her eyes and bit down hard on the strap. James took a deep breath, counted to three and made the first incision.

As the knife cut Wilhelmina's flesh, a strange sense of calm came over James. For perhaps the first time since Somerset left, he felt in control of his destiny. And that destiny was to save both Wilhelmina *and* her baby.

The midwife watched on in awe, astonished by James's unflappable calm in the face of poor Wilhelmina's screaming and squirming. She'd heard he was brilliant but this was something else!

James zoned everyone else in the room out, working quickly and carefully, and within just fifteen minutes, he had delivered what appeared to be a healthy baby boy.

'Is he all right?' Wilhelmina gasped. 'Please tell me he's all right.'

'He's more than all right,' James said, passing the squirming child to the midwife. 'He's perfect!'

But James's job was far from over. He still had the placenta to deliver and Wilhelmina's wound to sew up. He remained focused, taking care to make his stitches as small and neat as possible, explaining what he was doing every step of the way.

Around him, everyone was crying tears of relief and joy. James allowed them a moment to celebrate before ushering them out of the room, for Wilhelmina needed to rest.

'Champagne,' Mr Munnik cried once James emerged, happy tears streaming down his face. 'We must all have a glass at once! Dr Barry?'

'Later perhaps,' James said.

He didn't wish to ruin the mood, but Wilhelmina and her son were not out of the woods yet. Although they both appeared to be doing well, the next few days would be critical, especially for Wilhelmina, who was at high risk of infection.

'If I may, I'd like to stay and observe Mrs Munnik for the rest of the day,' he said.

'Of course, Doctor,' Mr Munnik said, his earlier doubts over James's medical judgement all but forgotten. 'Whatever you say.'

James ordered for the bedroom to be cleaned from top to bottom, and the bed linen changed. Once he was satisfied that the room was up to his exacting standards, Wilhelmina was allowed to return to the relative comfort of her bed to begin her recovery.

James remained with her for the rest of the day, and in the days that followed he made regular visits, until he felt confident that both mother and baby would survive. It was only then that he allowed himself to take in the scale of what he'd achieved – he was not only the first-ever British surgeon to perform a successful Caesarean section, but the operation was also the first successful procedure of its kind to be carried out in the whole of the Empire.

'Please, let me pay you,' Mr Munnik said. 'Let me show you just how grateful I am.'

James, although short of cash since his demotion, refused. 'I can't accept money,' he said. 'It wouldn't feel right.'

'What then?' Mr Munnik asked. 'You saved my wife and son's lives. I won't rest until I've repaid you in some way.'

James thought for a moment. His days at Wilhelmina's bedside had given him the chance to reflect on a good deal of things. Years ago, he'd made peace with the fact that he would never have a family of his own, or carry on the Barry family name, but suddenly here was the chance to alter that.

'There is something you could do,' he said.

'Anything,' Mr Munnik said. 'Just name it.'

'This might sound a little strange, but I wonder if you might consider naming the child after me.'

Mr Munnik agreed at once, christening the child James Barry Munnik and asking James to be godfather, a request which delighted James.

Word of the successful operation quickly spread. Journalists the world over wrote about it, congratulatory letters poured in from all four corners of the globe, and James was the toast of the town once more.

More than that, the successful operation ensured his name would appear on the pages of medical history books for centuries to come.

At the age of just thirty-seven years old, Dr James Barry was a legend.

WHAT
HAPPENED NEXT...

◆━━━━ ◆ ◆ ━━━━◆

THE LAST YEARS OF DR BARRY

BECOMING INSPECTOR
GENERAL OF HOSPITALS

I n the weeks and months that followed James's
successful delivery of James Barry Munnik, his
position in Cape society was restored. His earlier
indiscretions forgotten, he once more found himself
on the guest list of every fancy party in town, and
in November 1827, he was finally promoted from
assistant to full staff surgeon.

However, life had never been the same for James
since the Somerset family left the Cape, so when in
August the following year his posting came to an end,
he felt ready to bid goodbye to the place he'd called
his home for over a third of his life.

Following a grand farewell party, James boarded a
ship for a new life in Mauritius.

Over the next thirty years, he travelled the world as an Army staff surgeon, serving in Jamaica, Saint Helena, Trinidad, Malta and Corfu.

His habit of clashing with his colleagues travelled with him. In Saint Helena he caused such an upset during a dispute over medical supplies he was even arrested!

It was also in Saint Helena that gossip began to spread that Dr Barry might not be a man.

One day James was taking a bath when he realized one of his servants was peeping through a crack in the wall. Overcome with fury, he chased after her and beat her badly. Privately, the servants decided the severity of the beating only confirmed their suspicions – Dr Barry was indeed a woman. However, for whatever reason, they chose to keep the secret to themselves.

Several years later in Trinidad, after decades of being exposed to all manner of contagious diseases, James became dangerously ill for the first time in his life, coming down with a suspected case of malaria.

He was terrified. First of all, malaria was very often fatal. Secondly, anyone treating the disease would be very likely to discover his secret. James gave strict instructions that all medical intervention was banned and that none of his friends were permitted to visit him until he made a full recovery.

Unfortunately, two of his colleagues decided to ignore James's wishes and paid him a visit. Upon finding James fast asleep they elected to carry out a routine examination. Drawing back the sheets to listen to James's chest, the two doctors let out gasps of shock. At this, James awoke. Although sleepy and confused by their presence, he soon worked out what had happened.

'Please,' he said, tugging on their sleeves in desperation. 'Don't tell anyone of this, I beg of you.'

Although still in a state of shock, the doctors agreed not to utter a word. Indeed, they kept their promise and James's secret remained just that.

James's reputation for having a temper gathered momentum with every year that passed. In 1855, he took leave from his post in Corfu and travelled to Turkey. The Crimean War had been raging for over a year, with Britain and Turkey allied against Russia. James was keen to see its effects for himself. He began his visit at the Scutari Barracks in Constantinople, where Florence Nightingale and a team of thirty-seven nurses had been working for the past year. By now James was Deputy Inspector General of Hospitals and his arrival at the barracks was much anticipated.

The very first thing he did was tell off a young nurse for not wearing adequate headgear in the blazing sun, completely oblivious to the fact that the nurse in question was the famous Florence Nightingale herself! Florence was furious, later remarking that James was a 'brute' and the 'most hardened creature' she had ever met. James, of course, didn't care one bit.

In 1857, at the age of sixty-eight, James was given a new posting and a new title. He was bound for Canada where he would take up the post of Inspector General of Hospitals – one of the highest medical posts in the whole of the British Army.

James spent two years in Montreal, Canada before falling ill with bronchitis. He was granted temporary leave to return to England, unaware that he would never return.

Back in London, James was called before the Army Medical Department's board. They took one look at seventy-year-old James – weak, skinny and tired – and relieved him of his duties. James was shocked and devastated. He'd been so sure he was to return to his post in Montreal that he'd left behind almost all of his belongings! He appealed against the decision but to no avail.

James's career in the Army was over.

Over the next few years, James struggled to keep himself occupied. Unable to bear gloomy London, he went on holiday to the Caribbean, revisiting a number of his old haunts. In Bridgetown, Barbados, he met up with General Cloete, his old duelling adversary. Following their disagreement over forty years earlier, they'd become good friends. However, on this occasion James found himself clashing with a colleague of Cloete's, a gentleman named Captain Shadwell Clerke. Insults were exchanged and James, at the ripe old age of seventy, challenged Clerke to a duel. Luckily, Cloete heard of their argument and managed to dissuade the two elderly men from going ahead. James may have been physically frail but he was certainly as hot-headed as ever!

Back in London, James realized over thirty years had passed since his dear old friend Somerset had died. No one had ever come close to replacing him and those that had were all now dead too. With no social life to speak of and no work to distract him, James's days became unbearably long and empty.

Then, in July 1865, he became ill.

Very ill.

Fearing the end was near, he laid out clear instructions that upon his death there was to be no autopsy or any other form of examination. James's doctor and friend Dr McKinnon reluctantly promised to grant his request, oblivious to the real reason behind it...

TIMELINE

1789	Margaret Bulkley is born in Cork, Ireland.
June 1804	Margaret and Mary Anne move to London.
April 1809	John Bulkley joins the Army and Margaret decides to disguise her sex and train to be a doctor.
November 1809	James Barry arrives in Edinburgh to start his medical training.
January 1810	James studies anatomy and dissection with Dr Andrew Fyfe.
July 1812	James passes his final exams and is certified as James Barry M.D.
November 1812	James studies surgery at Guy's Hospital, London under Astley Cooper.
April 1813	James joins the British Army and begins work as a hospital assistant.
October 1813	James is promoted to acting assistant surgeon.
September 1816	James arrives in the Cape Colony.
January 1817	James tours the Cape with Lord Somerset.
October 1818	Somerset falls dangerously ill.
March 1819	James fights a duel with Josias Cloete.
March 1822	James is made Colonial Medical Inspector.
August 1825	James receives a court summons following his criticisms of the Cape's prison system.

October 1825	The post of Colonial Medical Inspector is removed.
March 1826	The Somerset family return to England.
July 1826	James performs the first-ever successful Caesarean section in the British Empire.
August 1828	James's posting in the Cape comes to an end.
September 1828	James is posted to Mauritius and given the title 'superintending surgeon'.
February 1830	Lord Somerset dies.
April 1831	James is posted to Jamaica where he is the sole staff surgeon on the entire medical staff.
July 1835	James is posted to Saint Helena as their Principal Medical Officer (he is later demoted to staff surgeon following his arrest in November 1836).
1840	James is made Principal Medical Officer of Trinidad. He falls seriously ill with a suspected case of malaria.
November 1846	James serves as Malta's Principal Medical Officer.
May 1851	James arrives in Corfu where he is made Deputy Inspector General of Hospitals. He is now the most senior first-class staff surgeon in the British Army.
October 1855	James travels to Turkey to inspect the treatment of casualties of the Crimean War.
January 1856	James returns to Corfu.

October 1857	James is made Inspector General of Hospitals and posted to Montreal, Canada.
May 1859	James returns to England where he is relieved of his duties.
July 1865	James falls ill and dies.
August 1865	The first news story about James's extraordinary secret life appears in a newspaper in Ireland. It hits newsstands in England the following week.

A LITTLE MORE ABOUT
DR BARRY'S WORLD

THE CAPE COLONY

The Cape Colony was located in what is now known as South Africa. The San and Khoikhoi people lived in its interior and the Khosa and Zulu people along its eastern seaboard. In 1652 the Dutch established a trading post on its southern tip, designed to offer refuge for Dutch ships during long voyages between Europe and Asia, and soon Dutch people began to farm the land, which led to conflict with the indigenous peoples. In 1795 the British defeated the French and took control of the Cape, and by 1825 English had replaced Dutch as the language of government, and the pound had replaced the Dutch rix-dollar, with increased immigration from Britain leading to further losses of land for the indigenous peoples. The Cape became self-governing in 1872 before uniting with three other colonies to form the Union of South Africa in 1910, a move that eventually led to the apartheid system (1948-1994), which made discrimination against the indigenous peoples the rule of law. Apartheid came to an end in 1994 but the social and economic effects are still felt today.

CAESAREAN SECTION OPERATION

Also known as a 'c-section', a Caesarean is the surgical removal of a foetus from the uterus through an incision in the abdomen and is usually performed if the life of the mother or child might be endangered by a regular delivery. It takes its name from a child from the ancient Roman family of Caesar born via this method. The first documented procedure on a living woman was performed in 1610. However, she died twenty-five days later. Many more attempts were made but the mother almost always lost her life, either from infection or bleeding. Improvements in surgical techniques, antibiotics, blood transfusions and antiseptic procedures mean that in today's society, the c-section is frequently performed as an alternative to regular childbirth.

DISSECTION

Thanks in large part to the Napoleonic wars in the first half of the nineteenth century, trained surgeons were in huge demand and the number of private medical schools soared in response. Almost all of them relied on a steady supply of dead bodies (usually obtained by a resurrectionist) for their students to practise on. If there were not enough bodies to go around, they would often be chopped up into pieces and shared amongst the students. Popular procedures included craniotomies (removing part of the skull to access the brain), thoracotomies (an incision to open the chest) and operations on the spinal cord.

DUELLING

A duel was a combat between two people armed with a lethal weapon, commonly swords or pistols. It was usually held to settle a disagreement or to defend a point of honour and was subject to a number of prearranged rules. Established in Western Europe in the Middle Ages when they were often used to decide legal disputes, duels became increasingly private affairs, often fought over the slightest thing. They fell out of favour in the early twentieth century with the last recorded duel taking place in 1967.

EDINBURGH MEDICAL SCHOOL

Although the University of Edinburgh's Faculty of Medicine was not formally set up until 1726, medicine had been taught at Edinburgh since the beginning of the sixteenth century. Its teaching was initially modelled on that of the University of Padua in Italy, and later, the University of Leiden in the Netherlands. Thanks to the creation of a teaching hospital, the number of students grew steadily and by 1764 the course was so oversubscribed that a new anatomy theatre had to be built to accommodate them all. Until World War One, the school was widely considered the best in the English-speaking world, attracting students from Ireland, America and the colonies.

LEPROSY

Also known as Hansen's disease, leprosy is a chronic infectious disease that affects the skin, the nerves outside the brain and spinal cord, and the mucous membranes of the nose, throat and eyes. For centuries, the disease was misunderstood with many sufferers shunned as 'unclean' and forced to live in isolated 'leper colonies'. In reality, leprosy is not highly contagious and, thanks to advances in medicine and therapy, it is entirely curable.

MIRANDA

General Francisco de Miranda was a revolutionary who fought to liberate his country, Venezuela, from

Spanish rule. Born in 1750 in Caracas, the capital city of the Spanish colony of Venezuela, he purchased a captaincy in the Spanish army but was disciplined for disobedience and forced to flee, first to the United States of America, then London, where he planned the liberation of South and Central America from Spanish domination. In 1811 he returned to Venezuela as a general in the revolutionary army and, when the country was finally declared independent, became its leader. However, the Spanish forces counterattacked, and when Miranda was forced to agree to a truce he was accused of treason by his fellow revolutionaries and handed over to the Spanish. They promptly transported him in chains across the Atlantic to Cadiz, Spain, where he died alone in a prison cell in 1816.

'RESURRECTIONISTS'

Resurrectionists (also sometimes known as body snatchers) were people who illicitly removed corpses from graves or morgues to sell to medical schools for use in the study of anatomy. Legally, only the remains of executed criminals could be used for dissection – but there were too few of these, so medical schools came to rely on the bodies supplied by the body snatchers, though it all had to be done in secret. The graves of the poor were preferred targets as they were less likely to be guarded. Jewish graveyards were also popular because the bodies were more likely to be fresh (Jewish custom dictates burial should take place within twenty-four hours of death). Instead of digging up the entire coffin, the body snatchers' preferred method was to dig a vertical tunnel, break open the head end of the coffin, then hoist the body to the surface using a rope or long metal hook. The Anatomy Act in 1832, and later laws, made dead bodies more readily available and by the 1880s there was no longer demand for the body snatchers' services.

SLAVES

Slavery was first introduced to the Cape by Dutchman Jan van Riebeeck, who first imported slaves from Indonesia, Mauritius and Madagascar before beginning to forcibly enslave Africans. Slaves in Dutch colonies were given poor food and forced to live in cramped, unsanitary conditions. Punishment by whipping was common. Upon taking control of the Cape, the British passed a law ending the external slave trade. However, it was still permitted to trade slaves within the colony. This practice was finally abolished in 1834, following the Slavery Abolition

Act of 1833, though many slaves did not escape their owners until 1840.

WOMEN AND MEDICINE

Today, women make up the majority of entrants to UK medical schools, but back in the 1800s things were quite different. Although women were able to work as nurses and midwives, they were either barred from attending medical school in order to train as doctors, or prohibited from sitting the examinations that would allow them to practise. A few women managed to take advantage of loopholes to get around the rules; later they campaigned against them. In 1874 Sophia Jex-Blake joined forces with a number of like-minded women to establish the London School of Medicine for Women – the country's first-ever medical school to allow women to graduate and practise medicine. However, progress was still slow. Only when World War One broke out in 1914, and the demand for doctors grew, did increasing numbers of women begin to study medicine – though gender discrimination against female candidates remained in place well into the 1970s when, finally, the application process was changed to judge candidates on merit not their gender. The number of women studying medicine has risen steadily ever since.

CALLING ALL TEACHERS AND EDUCATORS!

FREE ADDITIONAL RESOURCES AND MATERIALS FOR TRUE ADVENTURES CAN BE DOWNLOADED FROM

www.pushkinpress.com/true-adventures

INCREDIBLE PEOPLE
DOING INCREDIBLE THINGS

The most thrilling stories in history

BLUE MOUNTAINS, WINDWARD JAMAICA, 1720

High above the army camps and plantations of
the British Empire, a group of ex-slaves – called
Maroons – are building a new home for themselves.

When British soldiers enter the forest to hunt
them down, one of the Maroons will lead the fight
against them – Queen Nanny, a 'wise woman' with
a reputation for ancient obeah magic, and a guerrilla
fighter of genius. Under her generalship, her people
will make a do-or-die defence of their freedom.

NAZI GERMANY, 1942

As World War Two rages, Sophie Scholl reunites with her beloved brother Hans in Munich. Soon she meets his young student friends. Like her they can take no more of the war.

Then leaflets calling for a revolt against Hitler start appearing, put out by a mysterious group called the White Rose. Who are these people? No one knows. But the Gestapo is determined to hunt them down – and suddenly Sophie finds herself in the most terrible danger.

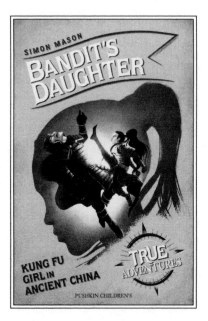

ANCIENT CHINA, THE YEAR 1000

It began with a duel. When General Yang wanted to get rid of a troublesome bandit, he sent his fiercest warrior: his son, Captain Zongbao. But on his way through the forest to find the outlaw, Zongbao unexpectedly encountered the bandit's teenage daughter, Mu Guiying – who challenged him to unarmed combat. And she was better.

The fight launched Mu Guiying's astonishing journey from fearless outcast to the great defender of her country, as she masterminded the Chinese defence against the invading horsemen from the north.